MUSIC IN THE CHURCH

MUSIC
IN THE CHURCH

BY

PETER CHRISTIAN LUTKIN

AMS PRESS
NEW YORK

Reprinted from the edition of 1910, Milwaukee
First AMS EDITION published 1970
Manufactured in the United States of America

International Standard Book Number: 0–404–04069–1

Library of Congress Number: 72–135722

AMS PRESS INC.
NEW YORK, N.Y. 10003

EXTRACTS

From the Will of the Rt. Rev. Charles Reuben Hale, D.D., LL.D., Bishop Coadjutor of Springfield, *born 1837; consecrated July 26, 1892; died December 25, 1900.*

 In the Name of the Father, and of the Son, and of the Holy Ghost. Amen.

I, Charles Reuben Hale, Bishop of Cairo, Bishop Coadjutor of Springfield, of the City of Cairo, Illinois, do make, publish, and declare this, as and for my Last Will and Testament, hereby revoking all former wills by me made.

First. First of all, I commit myself, soul and body, into the hands of Jesus Christ, my Lord and Saviour, in Whose Merits alone I trust, looking for the Resurrection of the Body and the Life of the World to come.

.   .   .   .   .   .

Fourteenth. All the rest and residue of my Estate, personal and real, not in this my Will otherwise specifically devised, wheresoever situate, and whether legal or equitable, I give, devise, and bequeath to "The Western Theological Seminary, Chicago, Illinois," above mentioned, but nevertheless *In Trust*, provided it shall accept the trust by an instrument in writing so stating, filed with this Will in the Court where probated, within six months after the probate of this Will—for the general purpose of promoting the Catholic Faith, in its purity and integrity, as taught in Holy Scripture, held by the Primitive Church, summed up in the

Creeds and affirmed by the undisputed General Councils, and, in particular, to be used only and exclusively for the purposes following, to-wit:—

. . . . . .

(2) The establishment, endowment, publication, and due circulation of Courses of Lectures, to be delivered annually forever, to be called "The Hale Lectures."

The Lectures shall treat of one of the following subjects:

(*a*) Liturgies and Liturgics.
(*b*) Church Hymns and Church Music.
(*c*) The History of the Eastern Churches.
(*d*) The History of National Churches.
(*e*) Contemporaneous Church History: *i.e.*, treating of events happening since the beginning of what is called "The Oxford Movement," in 1833.

It is the aim of the Seminary, through the Hale Lectures, to make from time to time some valuable contributions to certain of the Church's problems, without thereby committing itself to agreement with the utterances of its own selected Preachers.

TO THE MEMORY OF

John Harris Knowles, A.M.,

SOMETIME CANON OF THE CATHEDRAL OF SS. PETER AND
PAUL OF THE DIOCESE OF CHICAGO, THESE PAGES
ARE AFFECTIONATELY INSCRIBED.

TABLE OF CONTENTS

AUTHOR'S PREFACE

Bishop Anderson, when honoring the undersigned with the appointment of Hale Lecturer for 1908-1909, expressed the wish that the lectures might be made as practical as possible. Every effort has been made to comply with this request, and as a consequence, technicalities and discussions which would only interest the professional musician have been avoided.

The general plan of the lectures (which are printed as delivered) is two-fold: in the first place to set before the interested reader, be he clergyman or layman, a concise history of the various subjects, in order that he may arrive at an intelligent comprehension of the situation as a whole; in the second place to give practical suggestions bearing upon conditions as they exist in the average church or parish of to-day.

The writer is greatly indebted to the files of that invaluable journal for the Church musician, the "New Music Review" (published by the H. W. Gray Co., New York), for much detailed information and many pertinent suggestions.

Since these lectures were put in type an historical edition of "Hymns Ancient and Modern" has appeared. This book contains, in addition to the hymns and tunes, a history of the words and music in each instance, giving their sources and the original text in case of translations. The work is truly monumental in character and indispensable to the true hymn lover. A most valuable book, but concerning tunes only, is Cowan & Love's "The Music of the Church Hymnary and the Psalter in Metre."

The Bibliography at the end of this book, although far from complete, endeavors to give works covering all phases of Church music.

NOTE

The numbers in parentheses, under the hymn titles in the margin, refer to the hymn numbers in the authorized editions of the Church Hymnal.

I.

Hymn Tunes.

A consideration of the relative importance of hymn and tune opens a very wide field
for discussion, but as far as the general public Tunes, their importance.
is concerned the tune holds indisputably
the supremacy. Many a hymn of mediocre
merit has been sung into fame and widespread
use through the compelling power of the tune,
while many a worthy hymn has been unable to
survive inadequate musical expression. The
tune, therefore, becomes of vital practical
importance and it possesses qualities peculiar
to itself which no other agency can either displace or duplicate. It is the one channel
through which we can collectively voice our
offerings of prayer and praise to Almighty
God, the one medium by which all can unite
in an inspiring act of worship, and the only
means by which the people as a whole can be
swayed by a single emotion or uplifted by a
common impulse.

The tunes that are chosen for these high

purposes should receive serious consideration. It is not sufficient that they appeal to man, they must also be worthy of presentation to God. The question thus transfers itself to a higher plane than the mere pleasing of the individual taste. Fundamental worth, artistic merit, historic association, fitness as to time and place, practicability, are all factors which should be given due consideration in the selection of tunes. The important part hymn-singing has played in the development and propagation of the Christian religion should be told to laymen. Interest would surely be awakened by telling them of the historic value and associations of certain tunes, by calling attention to the fact that hymn-singing offers a common ground of unity even among the most antagonistic of Christian bodies. Moreover a precious bond of union with the past exists in those ancient melodies that were sung by the early Christians, melodies which are still in existence and are in use to-day in certain of our churches. The plainsong of the early Church, the chorales of the Lutherans, the psalm-singing of the Calvinists, and the development of hymnology in our own communion are all subjects of absorbing interest.

While we are indebted to our dissenting brethren in no small measure for the practice of hymn-singing in its modern sense, and also for many of our most beloved hymns, it is a notorious fact that with all their zeal for congregational singing no hymn tune composer of preëminence has ever sprung from the sectarian ranks. For nearly four centuries the Anglican Church has supplied English-speaking Christendom with its best tunes, tunes that are universally conceded to be models of their type. Their only rivals are the Lutheran chorales, but Lutheran hymnody is a thing of the past while the Anglican Church is to-day at its fullest and ripest period of musical expression.

We of the Protestant Episcopal Church of America are heirs to a rich heritage of hymn music and we share in the musical glory of our mother Church. Our hymnals are looked upon as models by other Christian bodies, and each denominational hymn book as it appears draws more and more largely from our pages. We occupy a responsible position in the development of Church music in this country, and it behooves us to maintain our high standards and to make no concessions to the musical fads and fancies of the hour. But we do not all realize our high calling nor appreciate the stores of treasures that we have to draw from. Education is needed all along the line; education for the layman, for the organist, for the choirmaster, for the theological student, and, I fear, for the three orders of the ministry.

Scope of lecture.

It is the object of this lecture to consider and discuss the musical material in our hymnals; to classify the better tunes; to give their sources together with a more or less critical estimate of their worth; and to explain their position in the evolution of hymn-singing. They will be considered in the following order:

I. Plainsong Melodies.

II. German Chorales.

III. Early English Tunes.

IV. Modern English Tunes.

V. American Tunes.

I.   PLAINSONG MELODIES.

Origin of plainsong.

The origin of plainsong or plain chant melodies is a matter of uncertainty. By some they are thought to be descended from the music of the Jewish Temple, and by others to be founded upon the musical system of the Greeks. In any event they present features utterly foreign to our modern scales and harmonic systems, and have such striking peculiarities that even the inexperienced readily recognize them. It is more than probable that the first Christians borrowed both music and liturgy from the Jewish synagogue, but as there is absolutely no authentic trace left of the music of the Jews it is impossible to verify the matter. It must be remembered that only since the tenth century has music been preserved by any definite system of notation. Previous to that time it was a matter of tradition, melodies being passed from generation to generation largely through the sense of hearing only. Curious melodies are to be heard in the modern Jewish synagogue which are claimed to be the original music of the Temple at Jerusalem, but they have doubtless suffered greatly through the mutations of centuries and the accumulated inaccuracies of aural tradition.[1]

Modern music is based essentially upon even pulsations and regularly recurring accents. Plainsong may be looked upon as an expansion of the natural inflections of the speaking voice in declaiming prose. Modern melody is fundamentally conceived upon a harmonic fabric, *i.e.,* it conforms itself to certain habits of harmonic progression and it is rarely satisfactory without accompaniment. Plainsong was written before the art of harmony was thought of, and properly should not be accompanied at all.[2]

Plainsong character-
istics.

---

[1] The tune usually sung to *The God of Abraham Praise,* and called LEONI (No. 460), is generally considered of ancient Hebrew origin. The words were written about 1770 and are an adaptation of the Jewish *Yigdal* or Metrical Doxology. The tune was arranged from a presumably traditional melody sung to the *Yigdal* by a cantor named Leoni, in a London synagogue. The melody as we know it has in all probability been influenced by eighteenth-century harmony, for it lacks the characteristics of great antiquity.

[2] If plainsong melodies be accompanied at all the harmonies should adapt themselves to the rules of modal counterpoint, a harmonic system which grew out of the

Greek
modes.

Furthermore, modern melodies confine themselves to our present-day modes, the major and the minor. Plainsong melodies at first had choice of the four original authentic modes of the Greeks,—the Dorian, the Phrygian, the Lydian, and the Mixo-Lydian, to which Pope Gregory the Great is popularly supposed to have added the four plagal or accessory modes. Later the system was expanded to no less than fourteen modes, which gave to plainsong an inexhaustible source of tonal variety.[3]

At first plainsong was syllabic—that is to say, one note was sung to each syllable—but it was not long before ligatures, or the slurring of two or more notes to one syllable, came into vogue. This principle was developed until it became a prime characteristic of plainsong, and long melodic phrases were sung to a single word or syllable. These "perieleses," as they were called, are frequently of great beauty and serve to give emotional expressiveness to the text. This expansion and development of the musical phrase was an artistic necessity, as custom permitted no text repetition. Similar extended

---

material of plainsong itself. The modern habit of accompanying Gregorian tones or plainsong melodies with sensuous chromatic harmonies and the free use of dissonances, is greatly to be deplored, and such treatment at once stamps the performer as utterly ignorant of the true nature and beauty of plainsong.

[3] A more detailed account of these modes, as well as of plainsong characteristics in general, will be found in the last lecture.

phrases were also sung to an inarticulate vowel sound and were called "pneumae."[4]

Although in the days of the early Church there was no sharp distinction between the sacred and secular styles of music, plainsong by its inherent strength, dignity, and beauty, as well as by its centuries of use, has fully established itself as peculiarly adapted to the purposes of musical worship. If we assume that it is desirable to have the music used for the worship of Almighty God something apart, something entirely removed from secular suggestion, then we are obliged to admit that even the tremendous development of the art of music in our day has nothing to offer more fitting, more characteristic, or better suited to its purpose than the ancient plainsong.

Peculiar fitness of plainsong.

------

[4] The following is the closing phrase in a twelfth-century *Kyrie* translated into modern notation:

It is surmised that the early hymn writers supplied also the tunes, but it is extremely unlikely that these melodies were original products. It is more probable that they were a species of religious folksong, made up of familiar melodic formulas and readily acquired by the people. In any event the early Church soon accumulated a rich treasury of Latin verse set to plainsong melodies of distinction and force.[5]

Lasting quality of plainsong.

That these melodies have lasting and vital qualities is amply proved by the few plainsong tunes that have come into general use. Take for example our well-known Advent hymn, "O come, O come, Emmanuel," to its plainsong setting. There are few tunes more universally liked or sung more heartily than this. And still it is a tune at which some experienced musicians look askance when first met with, because it is so far removed from the melodic and harmonic phraseology to which they are accustomed. While certain few never learn to like it, its general popularity is unquestioned. Excellent as this tune is, however, it is not a speci-

Veni Emmanuel (No. 45).

---

[5] During the various reforming and protesting movements these melodies came into disfavor, but many of the hymns were translated into the vernacular and supplied with new tunes. The plainsong tunes, however, remained in use among the Roman Catholics, and several hundred of them are still extant. It remained for the Oxford Movement of less than a century ago to discover and appreciate the real worth of these ancient melodies and to introduce their use into the Anglican Church. Since then their inherent worth has slowly gained recognition.

men of the pure plainsong melody. It is usually ascribed to a French Missal of the thirteenth century in the National Library at Lisbon, though thorough search has failed to reveal it. The tune is probably made up of a number of plainsong phrases, arranged to fit the metre of Neale's translation of the original Latin hymn, which dates from a Mozarabic Breviary of the twelfth century.

A more authentic example of the ancient style of melody is that of the *"Veni Creator Spiritus."* The original poem was written about the year 800 and the plainsong melody used in many of our churches has always been associated with these words. It comes with striking effect in the ordination and consecration services, when its venerable strains seem to emphasize the historic continuity of the priesthood.

Veni Creator (No. 289).

Here again we feel the force of a musical expression far removed from the musical idiom of our day and perfectly fitting the mediæval characteristics of the text. It must be admitted that modern settings of this hymn seem pointless and meaningless when once the spirit of the traditional tune has been fathomed.

Another general favorite is *"O quanta Qualia."* To hear this noble tune sung in vigorous unison is always an inspiration. Like all plainsong melodies, it appears to best advantage when sung by men's voices only. The

O quanta Qualia (No. 397).

tune sung to "The strife is o'er," by Palestrina, while not strictly a plainsong melody, has many characteristics of the early style.

These four examples exhaust the list of mediæval tunes that are at all generally known in our churches, but they suffice to demonstrate the great worth of these melodies and their practical adaptability to modern needs and conditions. Our ritualistic churches draw upon a larger selection from ancient sources, and melodies which at first seem to be "without form or comeliness" soon grow to be beloved.[6]

That there is a growing sentiment in favor of these tunes is attested by the fact that the last edition of "Hymns Ancient and Modern" (1904) has no less than seventy plainsong hymns, over three times as many as in the first edition of 1861. Immense labor was spent both on the translation of the text of these ancient hymns of the Western Church, and also upon securing the best and most authentic arrangement of the traditional tunes. These tunes are first printed in the ancient notation upon the four-lined C clef, with the square notes. Then

---

[6] Among the hymns most in vogue are *Pange Lingua, Corde Natus, Ecce Agnus, Stabat Mater,* and the beautiful Easter hymn, *O Filii et Filiae,* which, however, is comparatively modern, being of French origin and dating from 1674. *Pange Lingua,* dating from 570, is markedly characteristic of the plainsong type. Some modern editors attempt to force these unmetrical tunes into modern metres, a process which robs them of much of their distinctiveness. They should no more be governed by rigidly recurring accents than the free declamation of poetry itself.

follows a translation into modern notation, harmonized with proper modal harmonies, in case organ accompaniment is preferred. To quote the preface of the book, "No attempt has been made by bar or accents to indicate the rhythm, as in plainsong no strict time values are represented by the notes. The accent and character of the words must determine the rhythm and time of the music."

When one considers that twenty million copies of "Hymns Ancient and Modern" were sold in twenty years, the importance of this championing of the plainsong tune will be appreciated.

II. GERMAN CHORALES.

The Reformation brought forth marked changes both in the character and in the use of Church music. The Roman Catholic Church had developed a finely organized and highly elaborated system of music, founded upon plainsong, a system that remains to-day the embodiment of reverence and dignity, leaving little to be desired from a liturgical point of view. The more this early music of the Mass is studied the more apparent becomes its fitness to the ornate ritual of the Roman Church and to the language of that ritual. Unfortunately, however, the music was more and more relegated to the priesthood and officially appointed

Changes of the Reformation.

choirs, while the people's part both in the music and in the services generally was reduced to a minimum.

The Lutheran Reformation restored to the layman the right to join actively in the musical services of the Church. As a result thousands of hymns were written in Protestant Germany and these were provided with tunes which remain to-day an unexcelled type of congregational music.

The chorale.

These chorales, or hymn tunes, were the most characteristic feature of the Reformation music. Some of the earliest specimens were not "composed" in the modern sense of the term. In fact the word "compose" originally meant to arrange, or put together. At that period it was the fashion to develop long compositions, either vocal or instrumental, from a theme or *cantus firmus,* which was apt to be a fragment either of a plainsong or a folksong melody. These themes were frequently developed in a most elaborate manner according to certain set formulas. While this style of composition was at first very stiff and mechanical, it finally evolved into the masterly polyphony of Johann Sebastian Bach and became the foundation of the modern art of music.

Luther and his musical co-workers arranged the celebrated chorales of that period from folksongs, or from the music of the Roman Catholic liturgy. These melodies are in a sense like proverbs, and conform to that apt definition of a proverb, "The wisdom of many expressed by the wit of one." But whatever their source, these justly famous tunes are marked by devotional earnestness and great dignity. Some seem to have been hewn from solid rock, so strong and massive are they, while others are of a more intimate and appealing nature. The emotional element in music, as we understand it, was scarcely yet developed, and even the love song of Luther's time was a serious and weighty affair. When we recall this fact it is no shock to learn that the wondrously beautiful melody known as the PASSION CHORALE to "O Sacred Head surrounded" was originally a love song to the words *Mein G'müt ist Mir Verwirret.*

Martin Luther until comparatively recent date has been credited with a number of tunes as his own composition—notably EIN' FESTE BURG and LUTHER'S HYMN. Investigation seems to establish the fact that he, too, composed only in the sense of arranging and adapting. *Martin Luther, (1483-1546).*

As these chorales conform more nearly to our modern scales and harmonic system, they are much more easily learned and understood than the plainsong melodies. Like the latter, they are well adapted for unison singing on ac- *Chorales essentially congregational.*

count of the strong and diatonic (as opposed to chromatic) nature of the melodies. The early chorales were harmonized in an elaborate, contrapuntal manner, the intention being to have the melody sung by all the congregation, while a trained choir sang the harmonies.

Development of the chorale.

As was the custom in England, the melody of these German chorales was at first in the tenor part but was later transferred to the soprano part. The artistic development of the chorale reached its climax under the great Leipzig cantor, Johann Sebastian Bach, who introduced these already widely known and famous melodies into his oratorios and Church cantatas, and who harmonized them in a manner that established a model for all time. While of great beauty, these harmonizations are somewhat too difficult for ordinary use and simpler arrangements are better for the average congregation. It is rather a sad reflection on our vaunted modern musical culture when we are forced to admit that the art and workmanship of hymn tune writing in the time of Luther or Bach far excels the best efforts of to-day.

Ein' Feste Burg.

The compilers of our present official hymnal, through some inscrutable process of reasoning, have deprived us of the use of the most famous of all German chorales. They have made use of Buckoll's translation of *"Ein' Feste*

Burg ist Unser Gott," which changes the picturesque and irregular metre of Luther into commonplace eights and sevens, thus making it impossible to use the original tune. Consequently the tune known as LUTHER'S HYMN and usually sung to "Great God, what do I see and hear," is substituted. If the fine translation of Dr. Hedge had been made use of we should not have been robbed of the greatest of all hymn tunes, a tune that Heine called the "Marseillaise of the Reformation" and that Frederick the Great referred to—in all seriousness—as "God Almighty's Grenadier March." Bach has a Church cantata based upon it; Mendelssohn uses it in his Reformation symphony; Meyerbeer in one of his operas, and Wagner in his celebrated "Kaisermarsch," which glorifies the prowess of the German empire.

Of the thirty-odd tunes of German origin which are found in Hutchins' edition of our hymnal but one dates from the time of Luther. This is the one already referred to as LUTHER'S HYMN. This tune was arranged by the great reformer and music lover from a secular song and soon became wedded to Luther's own words, *"Nun Freut Euch, Lieben Christen G'mein,"* and the two were accounted to have made many converts to the Protestant faith. The tune first appeared in 1535 in Joseph Klug's "Gesangbuch."

Luther's Hymn (No. 37).

Contemporaneous with this tune and a most beautiful example of the quieter, more introspective style is the melody known as Attolle Paulum to the hymn, "Across the sky the shades of night." Both text and music are from the pen of the Rev. Nicolaus Decius, and date from the sixteenth century. The German words to this tune, *"Allein Gott in der Höh sei Ehr,"* is a metrical version of the Gloria in Excelsis.[7]

Mendelssohn, who, like all great composers, had respect and reverence for the traditional chorale melodies, uses this tune of Decius' in his oratorio of St. Paul. The melody is known as Decius in some hymn books and as Stettin in others.

The next tune in chronological order, Herrnhut, was published in 1599 and is sung to the Advent hymn, "Wake, awake, for night is flying." Both text and tune are accredited to the Rev. Philipp Nicolai. The tune is used with fine effect in Mendelssohn's St. Paul to a different translation of the same text, "Sleepers, wake! a Voice is calling."

The Passion Chorale, "O Sacred Head surrounded," first appeared in 1601 in its secular character. It was composed by Hans Leo Hassler and appeared as a chorale in 1613 to

_____

[7] This versifying of canticles and psalms became later a veritable craze, which reached its climax in England when the Acts of the Apostles were made over into metrical verse and duly provided with music by one Christopher Tye.

the German text, *"Herzlich Thut Mich Ver- langen."* It soon, however, became associated with *"O Haupt Voll Blut und Wunden,"* of which our hymn is a translation. Bach uses this matchless tune five times in his great "Passion According to St. Matthew." It is much in vogue in Germany to-day at funerals, intoned by trombones, and its sombre dignity never fails to make a deep impression. **Hans Leo Hassler** (1564-1612).

Our Palm Sunday tune, St. Theodulph, for "All glory, laud, and honor," was composed and originally written in five-part harmony by Melchoir Teschner and first published in 1615. Its vigorous swing and strong individuality have made it a great favorite. **St. Theodulph** (No. 90).
Melchoir Teschner (1600-?).

The most generally known, perhaps, of these earlier tunes, due no doubt to its sturdy straightforwardness and simplicity, is *"Nun Danket All Gott."* It was composed by Johann Crüger and dates about 1648. Mendelssohn uses it in his great cantata, "The Hymn of Praise." **Nun Danket** (No. 466).
Johann Crüger (1598-1662).

The tune Salzburg was written in 1652 by Johann Rosenmüller, a musician who at one time held the post of music director of the St. Thomas School at Leipzig, thus being a predecessor of Johann Sebastian Bach. The tune is sung to the words "At the Lamb's high feast we sing." It is a pity that a great chorale written about this period by George Neumark is **Salzburg** (No. 118).
Johann Rosenmüller (1615-1686).
George Neumark (1621-1681).

not in our Hymnal. It is variously known as Bremen, Augsburg, and Neumark and was originally sung to the German hymn, *"Wer Nun den Lieben Gott Lässt Walten."* This tune was such a favorite in Lutheran circles that no less than four hundred hymns were written to be sung to it in the course of a century.

We have now exhausted the older and more typical chorales to be found in our Hymnal, and they far exceed in beauty and real worth those of later date. For them to become popular is simply a matter of thorough familiarity, as the general public is by no means lacking in appreciation of good art when it has had fair opportunity of acquaintance. Every German is familiar with them and reveres them, and this love for these time-honored chorales remains when perhaps all other religious influences have vanished.

Of the remaining tunes from German sources we will find many sterling tunes but of a more modern character, and it will be difficult, in many instances, to differentiate between them and the better class of English tunes of the same period.

Heinlein, written in 1677 and associated with "Forty days and forty nights," still retains mediæval characteristics and is one of the few tunes in a minor key in general use. Ratisbon, dating from 1680, to "Bread of Heaven on Thee

we feed," is decidely modern in tone, as is also
MEINHOLD[8] to "Tender Shepherd, Thou hast
stilled." WINCHESTER NEW to "On Jordan's
bank the Baptist's cry" is from the year 1690
and is German, despite its name. The picturesque ELLACOMBE to "Come praise your Lord
and Saviour" is ascribed to 1700, but is probably a hundred years later. MUNICH, harmonized by Mendelssohn, associated with "O Word
of God incarnate," dates from 1701, and might
easily be considered modern English, but in the
fine Easter tune WORGAN to "Jesus Christ is
risen to-day" with its inspiring Alleluia refrain, we are back in Germany again and precisely two hundred years ago. "Come, Thou
long-expected Jesus" to STUTTGART gives one of
our best straightforward, everyday tunes and
the same characteristics apply to FRANCONIA
(1738), to the words "Stand, soldier of the
Cross," to SWABIA (1745), to "This is the day
of light," and to HURSLEY (1774), "Sun of my
soul, Thou Saviour dear."

Our greatest composers have rarely turned
to hymn-tune writing, but we have two fine examples from Haydn, LYONS to "How wondrous
and great," and the Austrian National Hymn
which is set to "Glorious things of Thee are

Meinhold
(No. 248).

Winchester
New
(No. 44).

Ellacombe
(No. 533).

Munich
(No. 284).

Worgan
(No. 112).

Stuttgart
(No. 48).

Franconia
(No. 210).

Swabia
(No. 28).

Hursley
(No. 11).

Lyons
(No. 467).

---

[8] Hutchins attributes this tune to J. S. Bach, but it appeared in the Lüneburgisches Gesangbuch in 1686, one year
after Bach's birth.

Francis Joseph Haydn (1732-1809).

Austria (No. 490).

spoken." Haydn had envied the English their national anthem, "God Save the King," and in consequence wrote the above-mentioned tune Austria in January, 1797. On the Emperor's birthday, February 12th, following, it was sung simultaneously in the national theatre in Vienna and the principal theatres throughout the provinces. Haydn was sixty-five years old at the time. Twelve years later, on May 26th, he assembled his household around him for the last time, and on being carried to the piano, played the hymn through solemnly three times. Five days afterwards he died.

Ignaz Josef Pleyel (1757-1831). Pleyel (No. 452).

Grace Church (No. 339).

Dix (No. 65).

The tune by Pleyel to "Children of the Heavenly King," and Grace Church to "O Thou to Whose all-searching sight," by the same composer, date from this period and are quite modern in style. Dix, a general favorite to "As with gladness men of old," dates from 1838.

III.   EARLY ENGLISH TUNES.

Characteristics.

The early English tunes are by no means as picturesque in outline, as extended in range, or as varied in character as the German chorales. They have as a class a certain rugged simplicity which adapts them admirably for general congregational use. The best example of this type is the familiar tune by William Croft called St. Anne (1708), to "O God, our help in ages past," and it is a fine example

William Croft (1677-1727).

St. Anne (No. 418).

of what a good Church tune should be. The melody is in convenient range of the average voice, which cannot be said of many of the German chorales. It is essentially dignified, nobly befitting the massive sweep of the text. It follows the early principle of plainsong, a syllable to a note, and the rhythm moves in stately strides of equal notes. The same composer's tune, HANOVER (1708), to "O worship the King" is another good specimen of this style. **Hanover (No. 459).** A tune of like character is DUNDEE, sometimes called FRENCH DUNDEE, to distinguish it from **Dundee (No. 417).** another tune of similar name, which was probably derived from a melody in Christopher Tye's metrical version of the Acts of the Apostles published in 1553. The FRENCH DUNDEE is nearly a century older than ST. ANNE, and first appeared in the Scotch Psalter in 1615. In Ravenscroft's "Whole Book of Psalms" (1621), it is indexed as a Scottish tune and is called DUNDY. It appears in some books as FRENCH, in others as NORWICH. DUNDEE is one of the best tunes of its type and was much used in the early days of metrical psalm-singing, being at one time one of eight authorized common metre tunes. These tunes were supposed by the ignorant to have been written by David, and they stoutly refused to sing aught but the tunes of David to the psalms of David. DUNDEE is used a number of times in our Hymnal and perhaps most generally to the hymn, "O God of Bethel, by Whose Hand."

The oldest English tune in common use is TALLIS'[9] HYMN (also known as TALLIS' CANON or EVENING HYMN) to "All praise to Thee, my God, this night." It is in canon form. A canon is a musical device in which a melody starts in a given voice and after a few notes are sung another voice starts the same melody and follows the first, the whole harmonizing together. It will be noticed that beginning with the fifth note the tenor sings the same air as the soprano, and that the missing notes in the tenor at the end will be found at the beginning of that part. In Tallis' time the four parts were known as "meane, contra-tenor, tenor, and bass," and originally the canon started in the tenor and was followed by the meane, or soprano. The composer gives the following quaint instructions regarding his nine tunes, which appear at the end of a metrical psalter printed in 1561: "The tenor of these partes be for the people when they will sing alone, the other partes, put for greater queers or to such as will sing or play them privately." It will be remembered that at this date it was customary to put the melody in the tenor part, and it would seem, according to Tallis, that the congregations in

---

[9] This is sometimes printed "Tallis's."

those days were no better prepared to sing in parts than they are to-day.

Other tunes of this period are TALLIS' OR- DINAL (1565), "In token that thou shalt not fear," and ST. FLAVIAN (1562), "Lord, Who throughout these forty days." *Tallis' Ordinal (No. 209). St. Flavian (No. 78).*

All these tunes use a syllable to a note, have even rhythm and simple melodies. The tune WINCHESTER OLD to "When all Thy mercies, O my God" is one of the oldest and dates from 1592. It differs from the English tunes so far mentioned in that it makes use of dotted notes. In England this tune is frequently used to "While shepherds watched their flocks by night" and is decidedly better than the tradi- tional tune to that hymn arranged by Sullivan. ST. MARTIN'S, which is sometimes used to the same text, is a type of florid melody which came much into vogue at the time of the Common- wealth and Charles the Second. It was a period of stagnation and decadence in Church music; anthems and services were prohibited; nothing but metrical psalms were sung; and the tunes were ornamented with absurd turns and trills. Trivial interludes were also played by the or- ganists between the lines of the hymns, thus disturbing their continuity. A relic of these times is still to be met with in Tallis' EVENING HYMN, which, in certain hymnals, has been dis- figured by triplets and passing or slurred tones. *Winchester Old (No. 657). St. Martin's (No. 54).*

America
(No. 196).

Henry Carey
(1685-
1743).

Adeste
Fideles
(No. 49).

Our national hymn, AMERICA, which we have appropriated from England, is supposed to have been composed by Henry Carey in 1740. At least it was first sung by him as a National Anthem at a public dinner in that year, and forty-five years afterwards the authorship was claimed for him by his son. Like WINCHESTER OLD, this tune makes use of dotted notes, but otherwise conforms to the simple early style.

No tune has been subjected to so much fruitless investigation as to its origin as ADESTE FIDELES or the PORTUGUESE HYMN. It received the latter name from the Duke of Leeds, who first heard it in the Portuguese chapel (R. C.) in London. It was ascribed by Vincent Novello to John Reading, a pupil of Dr. Blow, who was the master of that greatest of early English musicians, Henry Purcell. The date is given by Novello as 1680, and as this particular John Reading was born in 1677 there is evidently a mistake somewhere. Another John Reading was organist of Winchester College and died in 1692, but nothing suggesting the popular tune to "O come, all ye faithful" has been found among his compositions. As far as has been ascertained it was first published in 1782, but it was in common use in a number of Roman churches before that time, a MS. copy having been found dated 1751. As the tune is probably contemporaneous with ST. ANNE it is remarkable for its more flowing outline and the use of slurred notes. In fact it suggests the nineteenth rather than the eighteenth century.

From about the year 1750 an excellent type of tune was evolved which retained the sturdiness and manliness of the early type combined with greater freedom of melody and greater variety of rhythm. Fine examples of this style are DARWALL (1770), to "In loud exalted strains," by the Rev. J. Darwall; YORKSHIRE (also known as STOCKPORT and MORTRAM) to "Christians, awake, salute the happy morn," by J. Wainwright; and TRURO (1790), to "Arm of the Lord, awake," by Charles Burney. The two tunes by Webbe, ST. THOMAS to "Lo, He comes with clouds descending," and MELCOMBE (1782) to "New every morning is the love," as well as Barthélémon's MORNING HYMN to "Awake my soul and with the sun" revert to the earlier rhythm of equal notes.

Darwall (No. 482). J. Darwall (1731-1789). Yorkshire (No. 56). John Wainwright (?-1768). Truro (No. 265). Charles Burney (1726-1814). Samuel Webbe (1740-1816). St. Thomas (No. 39). Melcombe (No. 1). Francois H. Barthélémon (1741-1808). Morning Hymn (No. 2).

IV. MODERN ENGLISH TUNES.

The modern English tunes include all those written since 1800.

James Turle, who was organist at Westminster Abbey from 1831 to 1875, contributes two tunes, WESTMINSTER (1836) to "Lord, in Thy Name Thy servants plead," and ST. JOHN'S, WESTMINSTER (1863) to "According to Thy gracious word," which easily might be

James Turle (1802-1882). Westminster (No. 189). St. John's Westminster (No. 233).

mistaken for the product of a century or two earlier. The tunes of Henry J. Gauntlett are but a trifle more modern: St. Albinus (1852) to "Jesus lives! thy terrors now"; St. George to "Blest be the tie that binds"; St. Alphege (1852) to "Brief life is here our portion"; and University College (1852) to "Oft in danger, oft in woe." Samuel Sebastian Wesley, the grandson of Charles Wesley, and one of the best musicians of his day, supplies an especially fine tune in Aurelia (1864) to "The Church's one foundation." One would be disposed to say that it must have been written especially for the words, so perfectly do they fit, but it was originally intended for "Jerusalem, the golden," and the characteristic and altogether satisfactory tune of Ewing (1853) by Alexander Ewing that we sing to "Jerusalem, the golden," was written for the words "For thee, O dear, dear country," another section of the famous poem of Bernard of Cluny in praise of the heavenly Jerusalem. A good, vigorous, singable tune is Henry Smart's Regent Square (1867), to "Christ is made the sure foundation." That he can also interpret the quieter moods is shown by his popular and beautiful tune Pilgrims to "Hark! hark! my soul, angelic songs are swelling," and a fine sustained mood is found in his Nachtlied to "The day is gently sinking to a close." The harmonies to Nacht-

Henry J. Gauntlett (1805-1876).
St. Albinus (No. 122).
St. George (No. 672).
St. Alphege (No. 406).
University College (No. 506).
Samuel Sebastian Wesley (1810-1876).
Aurelia (No. 491).

Ewing (No. 408).
Alexander Ewing (1830-1895).
Henry Smart (1813-1879).
Regent Square (No. 483).

Pilgrims (No. 398).

Nachtlied (No. 7).

lied are richer and fuller than any of the English tunes thus far considered and they mark an important turning point in the evolution of the hymn tune. Up to this time tunes were rather general as to their mood or tone, and while many of them were written to some particular text, they could easily be transferred to other words of the same general character. Under Calvinistic influences religious verse in England busied itself largely with adapting the Hebrew Psalms to poetic measures. The result was very mechanical in its early attempts and confined itself almost exclusively with common metre. Then came a period of original work that was largely doctrinal or didactic, followed by poems of a missionary or evangelistic tendency. Hymns gradually became freer in their poetic expression and new combinations of rhythm appear. Finally the poetry of the Church took upon itself a more devotional and personal character, and these peculiarities called for like characteristics in the musical settings. The modern hymn tune, therefore, is of such an individualistic character that it is apt to be wholly satisfactory only in its original connection. The words and music, in the best instances, are indissolubly wedded together.

We feel this close union in the melodious setting of "Saviour, again to Thy dear Name we raise," by Edward J. Hopkins, called Bene-

Benediction (No. 32).
St. Athanasius (No. 385).

DICTION or ELLERS (1872) and also his ST. ATHANASIUS to "Holy, Holy, Holy Lord." Hopkins was organist of the Temple Church in London from 1843 to 1898, and during this long incumbency of fifty-five years he maintained

Tunes More Lyrical.

the highest standards of Church music both in selection and performance. In both Smart and Hopkins we note a more lyrical and emotional vein, which is typical of the modern hymn tune and which responds most intimately to the mood

Redhead, 47 (No. 348).

of the verse. Redhead's simple settings to

Richard Redhead (1820-1901).

"When our heads are bowed with woe" and "Rock of Ages, cleft for me" have this same

Redhead, 76 (No. 336).

feeling. The fullest development of this tendency, however, was left for two noted hymn-tune composers who were born within six days

John Bacchus Dykes (1823-1876).

of each other, John Bacchus Dykes and William Henry Monk.

Dykes was born March 10, 1823. Although in orders, he was a professionally trained musician and was at one time conductor of the University Musical Society at Cambridge. The degree of Doctor of Music was conferred upon him by the University of Durham. He confined his musical activities mostly to the composition of hymn tunes, of which he wrote about three hundred, and which, since his death, have been published in a single volume. Although unknown to the editors at the time, seven of his tunes which he modestly submitted were published in the first edition of "Hymns Ancient and Modern." Twenty-five more were added to later editions in which he assisted in the editorial work. Monk also was honored with the degree of Doctor of Music from the University of Durham and was organist of several London churches and of King's College, Cambridge, which has always been famed for its music. But he is more generally known as musical editor of "Hymns Ancient and Modern," and his taste and musicianship had much to do with the enormous success of that book. His contribution of thirty-five original tunes is by no means the least attractive feature of that model hymnal.

William Henry Monk (1823-1889).

Both of these musicians have qualities in common which place them in the very front rank of modern hymn tune writers. Their melodies are invariably of definite individuality, graceful contour, and above all things, singable. Their harmonies add richness and character to the melody, avoiding the commonplace on the one side and extravagance on the other. Their part-writing is masterful, each part in itself being tuneful and interesting. This is particularly true of the bass part, the deft handling of which is always the surest sign of ripe musicianship. Lastly, they both have a keen appreciation for the underlying thought of the text and

Dykes and Monk compared.

reflect in the music a faithful and concise composite of the meaning of the words.

Of the two, Dykes is the more picturesque, varied, and resourceful, while Monk's tunes have a quiet earnestness that is very appealing. At times their styles closely approach in their inner essence, as for instance, Monk's EVENTIDE (1861) to "Abide with me" and Dykes' HOLLINGSIDE (1861) to "Jesus, Lover of my soul." It would indeed be difficult to decide on the relative merits of these beautiful tunes, each is so perfect in itself, bringing out so adequately the tender trustfulness of their respective texts.

HOLLINGSIDE was named from Dykes' own home in Durham, where as minor canon and precentor of the Cathedral he lived for thirteen years. Later he was vicar of St. Oswald's. Monk is said to have composed EVENTIDE in ten minutes in a room where a piano lesson was in progress.

Monk is particularly successful when in a quiet, introspective mood, as is witnessed by his NUTFIELD to "God, that madest earth and heaven," his ST. MATTHIAS (1861) to "Sweet Saviour, bless us ere we go," and particularly in his communion hymn UNDI ET MEMORES "And now, O Father, mindful of the love."

That Monk can strike a more jubilant strain is manifested in his EASTER HYMN, "Jesus Christ is risen to-day," his tune ASCENSION to

"Hail the day that sees Him rise," his Coronæ to "Look ye saints, the sight is glorious," and his stirring Alleluia Perenne, "Sing Alleluia forth in duteous praise."

Coronæ (No. 130).

Alleluia Perenne (No. 462).

When we stop to consider the tunes of John Bacchus Dykes it is difficult to decide where to begin and where to end. Of the quieter, simpler tunes we have the graceful St. Agnes (1866), to "Calm on the listening ear of night"; the sombre but beautiful St. Cross (1861), to "O come and mourn with me awhile"; the pastoral Dominus regit me (1868), to "The King of love my Shepherd is"; the straight-forward St. Bees (1862), to "Jesus, Name of wondrous love"; the appealing St. Cuthbert (1861), to "Our blest Redeemer ere He breathed," and the bright St. Oswald (1857), to "Guide me, O Thou great Jehovah," named from the church where Dykes was vicar.

Dykes' Tunes.

St. Agnes (No. 55).

St. Cross (No. 105).

Dominus regit me (No. 412).

St. Bees (No. 149).

St. Cuthbert (No. 375).

St. Oswald (No.414).

Of a more vigorous type we have the ever popular Nicæa (1861) to "Holy, Holy, Holy Lord God Almighty"; St. Drostane (1862) to "Ride on, ride on in majesty," and the uplifting Alford (1875) to "Ten thousand times ten thousand," one of the very finest modern tunes.[10]

Nicæa (No. 383).
St. Drostane (No. 91).
Alford (No. 396).

---

[10] After the death of Dykes, Mr. Henry W. Baker, one of the projectors and editors of *Hymns Ancient and Modern*, wrote to the widow: "We are going to sing *only his* tunes to every hymn all next Sunday, and the *Dies Irae* after Evensong *for him;* followed by *Ten Thousand Times Ten Thousand.*" (Baker, by the way, wrote the beautiful melody "Stephanos" to *Art Thou Weary,*" which Monk harmonized.)

It is, however, in the opportunity for the picturesque or in the touch of the dramatic where Dykes' real genius shines. In his St. Andrew of Crete (1868) to "Christian, dost thou see them," we have almost a new type with its sharp and striking contrasts. The same method but in less degree is used in his beautiful Vox Dilecti (1868) to "I heard the voice of Jesus say," in his touching St. Sylvester (1862) to "Days and moments quickly flying," and in his dramatic St. John, "Behold the Lamb of God!" a tune which begins in the Middle Ages and closes rather all too sweetly in the nineteenth century. Among his best known and most widely sung tunes are Lux Benigna (1867) to "Lead, kindly Light," and his setting Melita to the hymn for those at sea.

Dykes' dramatic feeling, tempered by his keen sense of balance and propriety, has full sway in his Dies Irae (1861), and it is also another successful example of breaking the bonds of limitation in hymn music and hinting at methods which tend to enlarge the scope of congregational singing. Enough has been quoted from Dykes to prove that he is easily first among moderns in his art. In the preface to the collection of Dykes' hymn tunes, Sir George C. Martin, after enumerating some fourteen of the best known tunes, goes on to say: "They are 'on the lips of thousands,' and are associated with the most solemn moments of life. But because Dr. Dykes was happy in expressing emotions in a way that was intelligible to the masses, we must not overlook the real difficulty and merit of discovering a musical way to the hearts of men, for not every great composer has been successful with hymn tunes.''

In Joseph Barnby, Dykes has a formidable rival in popular appreciation. By many, especially professional musicians, Barnby is considered the superior. Barnby was somewhat of a free lance in Church music and vigorously defended his ideas. His position will be best understood through the following excerpt from the preface to his "Original Tunes to Popular Hymns," for use in Church and Home, published in 1869, and containing about fifty hymn tunes:

> "If the outward form into which these tunes have been thrown be likely to be censured, much more so I fancy is the modern feeling in which they are conceived. The terms effeminate and maudlin, with others, are freely used nowadays to stigmatize such new tunes as are not direct imitations of old ones. And yet it has always appeared strange to me that musicians should be found who, whilst admitting that seventeenth century tunes were very properly in what we may call the natural idiom of the period, will not allow nineteenth century ones to be written in the idiom of the present day. You may imitate and plagiarize the old

tunes to any extent, and in all probability you will be spoken of as one who is 'thoroughly imbued with the truly devotional spirit of the old ecclesiastical writers', but you are not permitted upon any account to give your natural feelings free play; or, in short, to write spontaneously. The strangest part of the argument, however, is this: that whilst you are urged to imitate the old works, you are warned in the same breath that to succeed is altogether without the bounds of possibility. The question then naturally arises, Would it not be better— though at the risk of doing feebler things— to follow your own natural style, which, at least, would possess the merit of truth, and to leave the task of endeavoring to achieve an impossibility to those who prefer it? For my part, I have elected to imitate the old masters in their independent method of working, rather than their works."

Fourteen years later in publishing a second volume of his "Original Tunes," a change in the public temper is apparent from the following remarks of the composer: "Happily no excuse is needed now for composing hymn tunes in the natural style and idiom, so to speak, of our own time. The modern hymn tune has long ago been accepted by all shades of religious opinion as a valuable aid to devotion. Nor has it been found less useful as a means of driving out the arrangements of secular airs which, from time to time, have threatened to make their way 'within the borders of His sanctuary.'"

The following paragraph is also of much interest: "I have endeavoured to record my sense of the unusual favor bestowed upon the first series by the musicians of America, professional and amateur, by setting to music nearly twenty hymns taken from the "'Lyra Sacra Americana.'"

While some of Barnby's tunes are preëminently successful, a certain number of them belong in the category known as "choir tunes," that is, tunes which on account of their harmonic complexity are ill-adapted for congregational use and better suited to a well-trained choir. Occasionally Barnby's bias for chromatic harmonies causes awkward or difficult intervals in the melody or the other parts and they require experienced singers to do them justice. Their difficulty does not necessarily militate against their abstract worth as contributions to modern hymn music, as they are no more complex than many of the German chorales of great renown, especially those which have been harmonized by Bach. But the chorales are intended for unison singing and the strong diatonic melodies are particularly suited to that purpose, while Barnby's tunes, as a rule, will not bear unison singing on account of a strain of elegance which borders on the effeminate.

From the musical point of view Barnby's work is unquestionably interesting, clever, and effective and as near originality as one could hope for in a hymn tune.   His harmonic phraseology, so to speak, is borrowed from the German and English part-song, and a certain expressiveness is gained thereby which appeals to the musician.   Nevertheless one feels a little the straining after originality and musical effect, and misses the whole-hearted devotion to the cause and the unselfish spontaneous expression of Monk and Dykes.   In Barnby one is apt to forget the words while enjoying the music, while in Dykes one is apt to forget the music in its perfect expression of the text.   One is religious music, the other musical religion.

If we compare settings of the same hymn by both Dykes and Barnby—and there are many such—a calm, dispassionate, and experienced judgment, taking into account both the literary and musical values, will pronounce for Dykes four times out of five.   Barnby seems almost to have challenged Dykes, for he has made new tunes to words which bore some of the latter's most popular settings. But he has not succeeded in displacing the beloved melodies to "Christian dost thou see them," "Holy, Holy, Holy," "I heard the Voice of Jesus say," "Jesus, lover of my soul," "Lead, kindly light," or "Come unto Me, ye weary."   On the other hand, it must be admitted that Barnby's Paradise (1866) is becoming a greater favorite than Dykes', and in

Barnby's tunes.
Paradise
(No. 394).

the burial hymn MAR SABA to "Now the laborer's task is o'er," Barnby has the advantage. While both have contributed settings to "Hark! hark, my soul," which appear in all the newer hymn books, neither has been as successful as Smart in his well-known tune. Barnby's fine SARUM (1868) to "For all the saints" is infinitely better than Dykes', but in entering the lists against the famous ADESTE FIDELES to "O come, all ye faithful," he is only partially successful.

A typical Barnby tune is ST. ANSELM to "O One with God the Father," but originally written for "O day of rest and gladness." It has a well-marked individuality and makes an effective processional. A similar but more striking tune is JORDAN to "O God, in Whose all-searching eye," originally set to "Sing to the Lord a joyful song." In his wedding hymn "O perfect Love" (called both SANDRINGHAM and FIFE) he strikes a more practical vein from the congregational point of view, and gives an excellent tune, full of warmth and feeling. HOLY TRINITY (1861) to "Lord, lead the way the Saviour went," and ST. ANDREW to "The Cross is on our brow" are good examples of tuneful, simple melodies. Barnby half apologizes for the chromatic harmonies in HOLY TRINITY by explaining that it was written for a

Mar Saba (No. 242). Angels of Jesus (No. 398). Sarum (No. 176). Barnby (No. 50). St. Anselm (No. 68). Jordan (No. 211). Sandringham. (No. 238). Holy Trinity (No. 270). St. Andrew (No. 212).

Adoro Te (No. 600).

Cloisters (No. 496).

Laudes Domini (No. 445).

Merrial (No. 535).

church where unison singing was adopted. ADORO TE, or as Barnby himself calls it, ST. CHRYSOSTOM (1872), to "Jesus, my Lord, my my God, my all," and CLOISTERS (1868) to "Lord of our life," both of which retain their original words, are fine types of modern tunes, being interesting from every point of view. One of his best and most distinctive tunes is LAUDES DOMINI (1868) to "When morning gilds the skies." This setting is most inspiring and would seem at first sight to be a "choir tune," but that it is not beyond the powers of many congregations has been amply demonstrated by practical use. An illustration of Barnby's emphasis on harmony is his much admired MERRIAL (1868) to "Now the day is over." The melody, it will be observed, in both the first and last of the four lines is entirely confined to one note, the interest centering on the movement of the alto, tenor, and particularly the bass. J. Spencer Curwen, of tonic sol-fa fame, in his interesting "Studies in Worship Music" decries this tendency to transfer the interest from the melody to the other parts. He gives a clever *"reductio ad absurdum"* of this principle by writing a tune consisting of repeated notes, accompanied by rather elaborate harmonies, and succeeds in making quite an interesting piece of music.[11] A closing and most

____

[11] Mr. Curwen's tune is as follows:

characteristic specimen of the Barnby style is his martial tune, THE GOOD FIGHT (1869), to "We march, we march to victory."

Barnby has unquestionably made real and important additions to our current stock of hymn tunes, and if he is open to adverse criticism in some respects it is only because "one star differeth from another in glory."

Sir John Stainer, who through his great ability and high ideals rehabilitated the music of St. Paul's Cathedral, London, has in addition to many notable larger works, given us some fine hymn tunes. One of his best is taken from his "Crucifixion" to the words CROSS OF JESUS (1887), and so named. This noble and dignified tune most admirably fits the words "In the Cross of Christ I glory," to which it is set. Like all his tunes, it has very solid qualities, suggesting a mixture of the German chorale, the early English style, and a strain of modern feeling. Another tune, OXFORD (1890), to "Lord, a Saviour's love displaying," is also from his "Crucifixion." His setting of "There is a blessed home" is suggestive of Barnby's influence. VESPER to "Holy Father, cheer our way," and CHARITY (1874) to "Gracious Spirit, Holy Ghost," have good, wearing, every-day qualities. The fine tune to "The saints of God! their conflict past" is called both BEATI

Margin notes: We march to victory (No. 514). — John Stainer (1840-1901). — Cross of Jesus (No. 359). — Oxford (No. 258). — Blessed Home (No. 679). — Vesper (No. 9). — Charity (No. 76). — Beati (No. 175).

and ALL SAINTS in Hutchins' Hymnal, but Stainer himself calls it REST.[12]

The tune in point, in its strength and straightforwardness, makes an acceptable setting for Kipling's Recessional. MAGDALENA to "I could not do without Thee," and CONTRITION to "O the bitter shame and sorrow" are both sterling tunes. Stainer's melodies have not the seductive curves of Barnby, nor the appeal of Dykes or Monk, but they have an inherent honesty and worth that will in time win general recognition. A collection of one hundred and fifty-seven of his tunes is published. *Magdalena (No. 603). Contrition (No. 612).*

There is one more prominent name in connection with modern English hymn tunes and that is Arthur Seymour Sullivan. His tunes are of somewhat uneven quality, certain of them being excellent, while others are but a close remove from the ordinary, but all are popular, as Sullivan is nothing if not tuneful. Among his better tunes are O BONA PATRIA to "For thee, O dear, dear country," ULTOR OMNIPOTENS to "God the All-Merciful," LUX EOI (1874) to the Easter hymn "Alleluia! Alleluia! hearts and voices heavenward raise," and ST. EDMUND (1872) to "Nearer, My God, to Thee," and *Arthur Seymour Sullivan (1842-1900). O Bona Patria (No. 407). Ultor Omnipotens (No. 198). Lux Eoi (No. 123). St. Edmund (No. 344).*

[12] This multiplication of names makes much trouble for the hymn-tune researcher. If the authentic name of a tune is not at hand, the average hymn-book compiler will invent a name of his own rather than go to any trouble in the matter.

Samuel
(No. 568).

Cœna
Domini
(No. 220).

Hanford
(No. 341).

St. Kevin
(No. 110).

Angel Voices
(No. 304).

St. Gertrude
(No. 516).

John
Baptiste
Calkin
(1827—).

Camden
(No. 253).

Calkin
(No. 208).

Sefton
(No. 454).

American
Tunes.

Lowell
Mason
(1792-
1872).

"I'm but a stranger here." His tune, SAMUEL (1874) to "Hushed was the evening hymn," is a gem of quietness and peace, and his Communion hymn, CŒNA DOMINI, to "Draw nigh and take the Body of the Lord," and his HANFORD (1872) to "Jesus, my Saviour, look on me" are both beautiful in their simplicity and expressiveness. On the contrary, ST. KEVIN, to "Come, ye faithful, raise the strain," his tune to "Angel voices, ever singing," and his world-famous ST. GERTRUDE (1872) to "Onward, Christian soldiers," are open to criticism for a certain "jigginess" of rhythm and cheapness of melody not associated with ideal tunes.

John Baptiste Calkin deserves notice for his characteristic CAMDEN to "Fling out the banner, let it float." The tune appears as WALTHAM AND DOANE in other books. The setting to "O Father, bless the children," and named CALKIN (also SAVOY CHAPEL) is a fine tune, as is also SEFTON to "Lift up your heads, ye mighty gates."

V.   AMERICAN TUNES.

Turning to America for good tunes we do not find a very extensive list nor many names of special prominence. The only tune-writer widely known to fame as such is Lowell Mason. His tunes, doubtless, filled a valuable purpose in their day and generation; and he rendered invaluable service in the promotion of choral singing, both sacred and secular, in the formative days of musical art in this country. Many of his tunes are becoming relegated to the past, but several of his melodies bid fair to live for some time to come. Two of his best known tunes, HAMBURG and OLMUTZ, are arrangements from Gregorian tones. His MISSIONARY HYMN (1823) to "From Greenland's icy mountains," his BETHANY to "Nearer, my God, to Thee," and his OLIVET (1833) to "My faith looks up to Thee," have crossed the ocean and gained entrance into many hymnals there. They are certainly excellent examples of tunes constructed from the simplest materials and deserve respect for their earnestness and adaptability to ordinary use. Next to Lowell Mason, William Batchelder Bradbury has been our most popular and prolific tune-writer. His tune, AUGHTON, to "He leadeth me," and ZEPHYR to "With broken heart and contrite sigh" will doubtless remain long in popular favor.

Horatio Parker, Professor of Music at Yale, represents the other extreme of American hymn music. He has contributed a number of noble tunes which are conceived in a broad style, and which, perhaps, look a little into the future with their bold harmonies and unconventional progressions. Hutchins' Hymnal, to which Parker acted as musical adviser, contains eleven of his tunes, while the edition of our Hymnal edited by Parker himself contains thirty. Like Stainer, Parker refrains as a rule, from writing new tunes to well-known hymns already supplied with tunes satisfactory alike to musician and amateur, and which have accumulated a traditional value. This fact confines a number of his tunes to texts that are rarely used or used only upon special occasions. For this reason they have but small chance to gain public favor. Parker is in his element when setting to music hymns of a grandiose style, and these he supplies with tunes of great breadth and striking characteristics. He seeks for rhythmical variety without loss of dignity, richness of harmony without loss of strength, and melodic originality without loss of grace. He delights in a bold transition in the middle of his tunes and indulges himself until it becomes almost a mannerism. Only rarely does he fall into familiar paths—a most difficult thing to avoid and not transgress the natural limitations of tune-writing.[13]

Foundation (No. 636). A characteristic example of Parker's style is his FOUNDATION (1894) to "How firm a foun-

---

[13] Parker's HOLY DAY to *Come, let us all with one accord* is curiously like Beethoven's tune SARDIS; and PRO PATRIA, to *God of our fathers*, suggests Harding's MORNING STAR. This, however, is only momentary, as it soon goes on its own way, and, gathering strength, culminates in a fine unison passage.

dation." This is a noble tune, finely balanced, and with an onward sweep that never wavers. Similar virile tunes but on more expansive lines are KING OF GLORY (1894) to "In loud exalted strains," and MOUNT SION to "O 'twas a joyful sound to hear." Other examples of masculine vigor are COURAGE (1894) to "Fight the good fight," AUBURNDALE (1894) to "Christ is our Cornerstone," and VOX ÆTERNA (1903) to "Hark! the Voice eternal." His dignified setting to "Ancient of days" (1903) will doubtless have difficulty in displacing Jeffery's popular but rather flamboyant tune to the same words.

King of
Glory
(No. 482).

Mount Sion
(No. 493).

Courage
(No. 505).
Auburndale
(No. 294).
Vox
Æterna
(No. 35).

Ancient
of Days
(No. 311).

The above examples are for the most part "choir tunes" and Parker has not hesitated to publicly criticise himself for the tendency to write for the choir rather than for the people. That he stands most distinctly for congregational singing has ample testimony in the following quotation from the preface to his own edition of the Hymnal:

> "In more than twenty years' experience as choirmaster the editor has not observed that improvement in congregational singing which is so earnestly to be desired. A school of hymnody, which many call sentimental, has grown up and flourished during the past twenty years without improving, so far as we have observed, either the quantity or the quality of congregational singing. We may almost be-

lieve that our grandfathers had better Church music for the people than we have. If we may accept the saying of competent observers, they had certainly more and better singing, under the influence of the singing schools in what may be called the later Lowell Mason time, in the form of service common to the most of New England, than is usually to be heard at present. But signs are now discernible of a desire for a healthier, sturdier, more manly feeling in hymns and tunes. These signs are unmistakable and widespread, and are most gratifying evidences of the improvement in public taste. Lovers of hymnody no longer seek sensuous pleasure in rhythm and harmony, desired naturally enough by the very young, but look rather for convincing earnestness and sobriety of feeling. Clearly we need not more tunes, but better ones, attaining a higher standard of musical worth and dignity."

Parker can also write tunes, and good ones, of a congregational character as witness his beautiful setting, Brannenburg (1903) to "More love to Thee, O Christ," his tender and simple Jesu Pastor (1903) to "Jesus, tender Shepherd, hear me," his graceful and appealing Stella (1903) to "All my heart this night rejoices," and his melodious Bude (1903) to "Thou Who with dying lips."[14]

From other purely American sources we have but little of real value or that promises to

Brannen-
burg
(No. 654).

Jesu Pastor
(No. 534).
Stella
(No. 538).
Bude
(No. 277).

---

[14] These four tunes, together with Vox Æterna and Ancient of Days, are in Parker's own hymnal.

be a permanent addition to our hymnals. We are indebted to Americanized Englishmen for some excellent tunes. Prominent among them is the Rev. J. S. B. Hodges of Baltimore, who came here in his early youth. His setting to "O day of rest and gladness," called HODGES, compares favorably with standard English tunes, and his Eucharistic Hymn, "Bread of the world," has moved many hearts by its earnest simplicity. The tune BRISTOL to "Hark! the glad sound! the Saviour comes," is by his father, Edward Hodges, who came to this country in 1838 and during his incumbency as organist of Old Trinity in New York, was the first to introduce the Cathedral style of service into this country. A most worthy successor to Dr. Hodges is Dr. Arthur H. Messiter, also English born, whose fine tune MARION to "Rejoice, ye pure in heart," has met with general recognition and use.

The composition of hymn tunes is at once the simplest and most difficult of tasks. Any tyro in the study of harmony can put together agreeable chord progressions allied to a singable melody, and amateurs are disposed to think that this constitutes a hymn tune. Such as these are turned out by thousands. Well worn phrases from good tunes are revamped after the manner of a rag-carpet, and their very familiarity, which breeds contempt in the musician, gives them a popular vogue, for they are both easy to learn and easy to sing. Fortunately the cheap tune is usually associated with cheap words, and our Church is saved from a deluge of inanity both in words and music by its wise provision which permits nothing but duly authorized hymns to be sung. While we thus escape the maudlin sentiment of the Gospel hymn-tune we are by no means free from the musical **Amateur dabblers.** upstart who cannot appreciate sterling worth, and to whom the value of tradition is nothing. He feels called upon to write new tunes to our most treasured hymns, and worse still, he succeeds in having them sung; and not infrequently they find their way into standard hymnals. They are always "taking" in the popular sense, and apt to have sensational features. Processional hymns are the favorites, for a marching rhythm makes the first appeal to elementary musical instincts. A formula for such a tune would consist of a jingling rhythm recurring with deadly regularity, a melody gaily moving along the line of least resistance, and a few "barber shop" chords to help out the climax, which will be greatly heightened if some of the sopranos sustain a high tone in the refrain—for there must be a refrain! People will publish tunes who would not dream of publishing verse, and still they know infinitely more of the rules of grammar, rhetoric, and poetic rhythm than they know of harmony or composition.

A good tune is most difficult to write because within very circumscribed limits something definite and characteristic must be expressed. While comparatively simple material must be used, it should neither be commonplace nor reminiscent. The parts must be in convenient range of the different voices. The harmonic frame must not be too elaborate for the melodic picture. It must be concise, logical, artistic, and well-balanced. It must have sentiment without sentimentality, dignity without angularity. It is not surprising, then, that one of the foremost of American composers when invited to contribute to the hymnal of a leading denomination declined with thanks, excusing himself on the ground that he would rather write a sonata than a hymn tune! *Difficulties in good tune writing.*

While it is true that our greatest composers have rarely turned their attention to hymn-tune writing, it is equally true that our best tunes have been written invariably by trained musicians who, at the same time, were earnest, devout Christians. And this suggests the query, Is not the first requisite of the Church composer a reverent spirit: reverence for the Christian religion, reverence for literary values, reverence for musical expression? *Best tunes by trained musicians.*

The criticism aimed at the amateurish dab- *Professional dabblers.*

bler in hymn-tune writing also holds good in many instances in the profession, for many musicians dash off wretched hymn tunes who are excellent performers, teachers, or choirmasters but who have had no special training in composition or in the ethics of good Church music. A most curious contradiction is the fact that musicians who have the highest standards when judging the work of others and whose ideals and taste are unquestioned, seem to lose their viewpoint entirely when they take their pen in hand, and perpetrate a kind of music they would not tolerate in others.

If these would-be Church composers would stop to consider that the language of the Scriptures and of the Prayer Book are models of purity and refinement, that the hymns in use with us are for the most part the work of trained and scholarly minds, and that anything short of these high standards would be unseemly to offer to Almighty God, they might perhaps realize that music as a worthy consort deserves equally serious consideration.

Essentials of a good tune. A good tune is judged by precisely the same standards as a good hymn. The thought must be worthy, the expression adequate, the workmanship above criticism, and the artistic sense apparent. Logic, order, proportion, and perspective must all be there, as well as an assuring sense of mastery in all the details. If we are to wed music to worthy words the work of composition is not to be entered into unadvisedly, but reverently, discreetly, and in the fear of the Lord.

This chapter will best be brought to a close by a quotation from that admirable and most suggestive book, "Musical Ministries in the Church," by Waldo Selden Pratt, Professor of Music in the Hartford Theological Seminary. Professor Pratt sums up the situation in the following appreciative way, and one scarcely knows which to admire the more, his broad and sure grasp of the whole question, or the beauty and completeness of his powers of expression:

"Our Christian hymns are surely among the most powerful agencies we have for developing the religious sentiment of our people. The best of them are exquisitely beautiful in form and imagery, are magnetic and noble in tone and spirit, and deal habitually with topics and aspects of truth that all lie close to the heart of the Gospel. As a rule, they spring out of religious experience at its best and they tend to lift experience to its highest levels. The very cream of truth and of soul-life is gathered into them. They contain the refined riches, the precious essences, the cut and polished jewels of Christianity in all the ages. They tend to be superlative and ideal in both thought and expression, simply because so often they come from souls of rare endowment and unusual spiritual attainment. They therefore push on far beyond what most of us could perhaps ourselves say in sober truth. But they proclaim and represent nothing but what in our hearts we long for and aspire unto. They often ascend into the realm of ecstacy, and speak as of seeing the invisible and participating in the inaccessible. Herein they are truly prophetic, the records of the insight and intuition and rapture of seer and saint. These sublime qualities, of course, are not possessed by all hymns, but they mark so many that in these days it is possible for practical hymn-singing to confine itself to such continually if it chooses.

"It is by no means as commonly seen as it ought to be that entirely parallel claims may safely be made for much of the tune music that belongs to our hymns. The best of it, especially in recent periods, is as beautifully articulated as the finest sonnets or the most exquisite miniatures, is rich and thrilling in total effect, and is charged at every point with the same spiritual intensity as the hymns that have called it forth. Most of our finer tunes are written by men of devout character and sympathies, and are plainly marked by religious fervor and elevation. If we accord the praise of being true revelators to Wesley, Cowper, Montgomery, Bishop How, Ellerton, Ray Palmer, and many others of the same high rank, we should be ready to give similar acknowledgment to the scores of musical artists who have wrought side by side with them in the same noble ministry, like Gauntlett and Dykes and Barnby and Sullivan and Stainer, not to name others of other schools. Popular appreciation of the interior beauty and nobility

of tunes falls behind that of the value of
hymns simply because of popular ignorance,
and even musical critics are often perversely
blind to the triumph involved in writing a
really excellent hymn tune. Sooner or later,
however, the one will be valued not less than
the other."

II.

Congregational Singing.

The hymn-singing of the Christian Church had its roots in the psalmody of the Hebrew people, and it is the purpose of this paper to trace in a cursory manner its development through the crude but elaborate music of the Jews, the hymn singing of the early Christians, the plainsong of the Roman Catholic Church, the chorales of the Lutherans, the psalm singing of the Calvinists and Puritans, and the spiritual songs of the Wesleyans, as well as through the practice of our own Church, until we arrive at modern hymnody, which will receive special consideration as to its meaning and application to the Protestant Episcopal Church of America.

I. HISTORY OF HYMNODY.

In Exodus 15 we read as follows:

Hebrew
music.

> "Then sang Moses and the children of Israel this song unto the Lord, and spake, saying, I will sing unto the Lord, for He hath triumphed gloriously: the horse and his rider hath He thrown into the sea.

"And Miriam the prophetess, the sister of Aaron, took a timbrel in her hand; and all the women went out after her with timbrels and with dances.

"And Miriam answered them, Sing ye unto the Lord, for He hath triumphed gloriously: the horse and his rider hath He thrown into the sea."

While we are uncertain as to the precise meaning of the word "singing" in the above quotation (for the term may have signified naught but a shouting or crude chanting), yet it seems quite possible that congregational singing in well-defined melodies was a settled habit among the Hebrews, even in the time of Moses and Miriam, for the lifting up of the voice of the populace in song was doubtless a primitive instinct in the heart of man. But it was not alone in vocal strains that Israel praised the Lord, for we read in the account of the procession of the Ark that "David and all Israel played before God with all their might, and with singing, and with harps, and with psalteries, and with timbrels, and with cymbals, and with trumpets." (I. Chron. 13: 8.)

To prepare for the Temple service there was formulated an elaborate musical plan enlisting no less than 4,000 singers and players, all of whom were probably males. This vast body was under the instruction of 288 skilled musicians and a head precentor or "master of song."

At the dedication of the Temple we read the following interesting account of the music in II. Chron. 5:12:

> "Also the Levites which were the singers, all of them of Asaph, of Heman, of Jeduthun, with their sons and their brethren, being arrayed in white linen, having cymbals and psalteries and harps, stood at the east end of the altar and with them an hundred and twenty priests sounding with trumpets.

> "It came even to pass, as the trumpeters and the singers were as one, to make one sound to be heard in praising and thanking the Lord: and when they lifted up their voice with the trumpets and cymbals and instruments of music, and praised the Lord, saying, For He is good: for His mercy endureth forever: that then the house was filled with a cloud, even the house of the Lord."

The account establishes beyond a doubt the great importance attached to music by the Jews. We might infer that with the development of an official band of performers, the participation of the people in the services of the inner Temple was more or less restricted. In the outer courts, however, it seems that congregational singing was more generally cultivated, the voices of women and children joining in the popular celebrations.

The extensive use of instruments, the trumpets for interludes, the pipes and stringed instruments for accompaniments, the cymbals to mark the rhythm, all go to indicate a considerable development in concerted music. Then again the psalms are unquestionably intended for the purposes of song. The very nature of their parallel construction at once suggests antiphonal singing, either between precentor and congregation, or between answering choirs.[1]

As to the character of the music of the Jews we are quite ignorant. The accent marks which exist in ancient manuscripts are supposed to have been guides or helps to the singers in remembering the melodies. Their exact use has never been solved, and it is extremely doubtful if a solution to their mystery will ever be found. The music may have been of the most primitive character, consisting of chant-like intonations and cadences; or, as some Jewish authorities contend, it may have been of a more developed nature and the germ or source of the plainsong music that rose to such heights of beauty and perfection in the Latin Church. Traditional melodies which the Jews claim as authentic Temple music are still to be heard in the synagogues of to-day, but these melodies vary widely in different countries, agreeing only in certain

Character of Hebrew music.

------

[1] The psalms constitute an inexhaustible mine of riches for the musical composer down to the present day, and excerpts from them form the text of our greatest anthems and cantatas. They occupy an important place in the liturgy of all Christian Churches, and in their metrical version they are an important part of our hymnody.

peculiar melodic progressions which are unmistakably of Oriental origin.

In the first centuries of Christianity we find an exact parallel to the development of music as it occurred among the Jews. Before the crystallization of forms of worship in the early Church the people joined universally and heartily in the singing of the psalms and hymns. This was following the injunction of St. Paul (Eph. 5:19; Col. 3:16) in "Speaking to yourselves in psalms and hymns and spiritual songs." As St. Paul makes this triple allusion in his letters both to the Ephesians and the Colossians it is thought that in "psalms" he refers to the psalms of the psalter, in "hymns" to the canticles of the Old Testament, and in "spiritual songs" to hymns composed by the Christians themselves.

We read of the early Christians assembling before daylight and singing hymns alternately to Christ, and of employing in their meetings "two choirs, one of men and one of women. From each of these a person of majestic form was chosen to lead. These then chanted hymns in honor of God, composed in different measures and modulations, now singing together, and now answering each other by turns." This last practice suggests the antiphonal music of the Jews, from whom it was no doubt derived. That the music was not always of the simplest or most suitable character is indicated by the action of Clement of Alexandria (died 220 A. D.) who forbade the use of certain melodies because of chromatic intervals.

Later on the Church authorities were obliged in self-defence to confine the singing of the people to certain psalms and canticles and to interdict the promiscuous singing of hymns, as it was such a fruitful source of spreading sedition and heresy. *Hymn singing a source of heresy.*

In Gibbon we read:

"The Arians had been forbidden by the Emperor Theodosius to have places of worship within the city. But on Saturdays and Sundays and great festivals they were in the habit of assembling outside the gates, then coming into the city in procession at sunset, and all night, in the porticoes and open places, singing Arian hymns and anthems with choruses. Chrysostom feared that many of the simple and ignorant people would be drawn from the faith. He therefore organized nightly processions of orthodox hymn-singers, who carried crosses and lights, and with music and much pomp rivalled the efforts of the heretics. Riots and bloodshed were the consequence. Very soon an Imperial edict put a stop to Arian hymn-singing in public. The use, however, of hymns in nocturnal services of the Church became established."

Congregational singing was thus in general use in the early days of the Church, but, as was the case in the Temple music, with the develop- *Congregational singing in the Roman Church.*

ment of the liturgy and ritual of the Roman Church and the perfecting of their ecclesiastical organization, the people's part in the services was finally reduced to a few responses. The singing of the psalms, canticles, hymns, and Mass numbers was entrusted to trained choristers who were ecclesiastics of a minor order, and thus the performance of music in the Roman Church became largely a clerical function. Hymn-singing in all probability continued to be indulged in by the laity in the home circle, in private worship, and perhaps at special popular religious functions.

A hymn as defined by St. Augustine. St. Augustine thus defines a hymn: "Hymns are the praise of God with song; hymns are songs containing the praise of God. If there be praise and it be not God's praise, it is not a hymn. If there be praise and that God's praise, and it be not sung, it is not a hymn. To constitute a hymn, then, it is necessary that there be these three things: praise, the praise of God, and song."

Under this definition psalms and special acts of praise, such as the Gloria in Excelsis, the Magnificat, etc., were termed hymns. The hymn referred to as sung by our Lord and His Apostles at the Last Supper was doubtless the Hallel, which included Psalms 113th to the 118th, and it is quite possible that the psalm "When Israel **Tonus Peregrinus.** came out of Egypt," was sung to the Peregrine tone, a Gregorian which is used to this day in many of our churches and which has been associated with that psalm since the earliest musical records. The Te Deum is frequently referred to as the Ambrosian hymn, and tradition has it that at the baptism of St. Augustine on Easter night, 387, St. Ambrose and his distinguished convert improvised the great hymn in alternate strophes. The Te Deum, however, is of Greek origin in all probability.

Te Deum.

Metrical hymns in the modern sense of the word were not fully developed until about the fifth century, and St. Ambrose is credited with their introduction into the Western Church. They became very popular in the succeeding centuries, a vast number being written by monks and priests of the Roman communion. Of these some 3,500 have been traced and catalogued by specialists in hymnody. Some of our best known hymns come from the mediæval Latin Church poets, such as "Jerusalem, the golden," "For thee, O dear, dear country," "Brief life is here our portion," "Jesus, the very thought of Thee," "Come, Holy Ghost, our souls inspire," "O Sacred Head surrounded," "The day is past and over," and many others.

Metrical hymns.

Mediæval Latin hymns.

When the Christian religion invaded Germany the Roman Church authorities found themselves compelled to reckon with the innate love of the German people for music. This love

Congregational singing in Germany.

had long expressed itself in "folk-songs," both in their secular and religious relations. As early as 1195 we read of a choral society being formed in Prague for the study of spiritual songs, and in the thirteenth century popular songs were permitted at certain church festivals. But this was a far cry from the personal approach to God encouraged by Luther. When he maintained the right of laymen to participate in public worship and to praise God through their beloved medium of song and in their native tongue, the enthusiasm of the people knew no bounds. This sudden liberty on the part of the people to freely express their religious emotions, combined with the assurance of salvation by faith alone without priestly intervention, resulted in a veritable flood of verse and melody. It is estimated that over one hundred thousand hymns have been written in Protestant Germany alone, and their accompanying chorale melodies number many thousands. It is claimed that the hymn-singing made many more converts to the German Evangelical Church than did the preaching.

Lutheran hymns.

The German chorale.

The intense love of Luther for music and his practical knowledge of the art, together with the innate musical nature of his followers and their reverent attitude toward religion, all combined to evolve a type of hymn tune which for dignity, breadth, and fundamental worth has remained unexcelled. Skilled musicians busied themselves with arranging and composing melodies, and their efforts resulted in such a high standard of attainment, and such a corresponding elevation of public taste, that the Lutheran Church has never suffered from trashy or unworthy hymn music.

With the Calvinists it was quite different. They looked upon the efforts of man as an unfit offering to Almighty God, and they therefore confined their singing to metrical versions of the psalms of David. As to music, Calvin expressed himself as follows: "Those songs and melodies which are composed for the mere pleasure of the ear, and all they call ornamental music, and songs for four parts, do not behoove the majesty of the church, and cannot fail to greatly displease God." In consequence the tunes selected were of a sober not to say a forbidding character. Like many of the German chorales, the melodies set to the Genevan Psalter (as the official Calvinistic psalm-book was called) were taken from folk-songs, but of French origin. The most famous of these tunes is that known as OLD HUNDRED, which was originally sung not to the hundredth but to the one hundred and thirty-fourth psalm. A visitor to Geneva in 1557 gives the following account of the psalm-singing of the Calvinists:

"A most interesting sight is offered in the

city on the week days, when the hour of the sermon approaches. As soon as the first sound of the bell is heard all shops are closed, all conversation ceases, all business is broken off, and from all sides the people hasten into the nearest meeting house. There each one draws from his pocket a small book containing the psalms with notes, and out of full hearts, in the native speech, the congregation sings before and after the sermon. Every one testifies to me how great consolation and edification is derived from this custom."

Psalm singing of Puritans.

Calvin's abhorrence of ritual and his detestation of art in any of its manifestations as an adjunct to religion, including both organ and choir, found sympathetic response in both the English Puritans and the Scotch Presbyterians. Many English Protestants, during the religious persecution of Mary, fled to Geneva, where they fell under the influence of Calvin. Upon their return to England they brought with them the psalm-singing habit. Metrical psalms at once sprang into enormous favor, not only with the Nonconformists but in the Established Church as well. Would-be poets not only versified the psalms, but the canticles, the Creed, the Lord's Prayer, and a considerable portion of the New Testament in addition. A semi-official version of the psalms appeared in 1562 under the title:

Sternhold and Hopkins Psalm-book.

"The Whole Booke of Psalmes collected into English metre, by T. Sternhold, J. H.

Hopkins, and others, conferred with the Ebrue, with apt notes to sing them withal. Set forth and allowed to be sung in all churches, of all the people together, before and after Evening Prayer, and also before and after sermons, and moreover in private houses for their godly solace and comfort, laying apart all ungodly songs and ballads, which tend only to the encouraging of vice and the corrupting of youth."

The Sternhold and Hopkins version, known later as the "old version," despite its crudeness and literalness, enjoyed immense popularity and was not displaced until 1696, when the "new version" by Tate and Brady came into use, a version which sacrificed the ruggedness of Sternhold and Hopkins for weaker, if more graceful lines. Next in turn came Watts' version to which he gave the title "Imitation of the Psalms of David in the Language of the New Testament." This version was of a much higher order of literary and poetic merit and became popular with the dissenters. In the meantime, the Scotch Presbyterians had replaced their first Psalter (a combination of the Genevan Psalter, Sternhold and Hopkins and original paraphrases) by Rous' Version, which appeared in 1650 and met with great favor.[2]

Tate and Brady.

Watts' version.

Rous' version.

---

[2] It may be of interest to add that the Genevan Psalter passed through at least a thousand editions; that it was translated into the Dutch, German, Italian, Spanish, Bohemian. Polish. Latin, and Hebrew Languages, and was used even by the Roman Catholics. Julian, in his "Dictionary of Hymnology," gives a list of 326 versions of the entire 150 psalms in the English language alone.

Ainsworth's version.

The Puritans brought with them to this country a version by Ainsworth, while the Church of England adherents remained faithful to Sternhold and Hopkins. In 1636 a committee of Congregationalists prepared an original transcription of the psalms into verse known as **Bay Psalm-book.** the Bay Psalm-book, and later as the New England Version.[3] Owing to a scarcity of books **"Lining out" or "deaconing."** there arose the custom of "lining out" the metrical psalms in New England, and a device more fatal to musical effect could hardly be imagined. Each line of the psalm was first read over by the clerk or minister and then sung by the congregation. The music was thus broken up into disconnected fragments and was apt to lose its identity. In fact it not infrequently happened that a congregation became "side-tracked" and ended with a tune other than the one "pitched" at the start. The only argument in favor of this unhappy custom was the fact that it permitted the introduction of new hymns without the expense of printing them, and it was no doubt due to this habit that Watts wrote a new hymn for over two hundred consecutive Sundays. So ingrained was this custom of "lining out" that it was continued even after the hymns were thoroughly familiar to all the congregation.

A word as to the tunes used to the metrical

---

[3] This passed through seventy editions.

psalms. The Sternhold and Hopkins Psalter of 1562 contained forty tunes, mostly in common metre, for all but twenty of the one hundred and forty psalms were in that metre. The melody only was printed and the tunes were of rather a severe type, Old Hundred and Dundee being samples. The Scotch Psalter of 1635 contained one hundred and forty-three tunes from French, English, and German sources. Among the dissenters the tunes gradually grew less in number until in some communities they were reduced to six or eight in number, and these attained such a traditional and sentimental value among the ignorant that it was considered almost heretical to use other music. This restricted repertoire of tunes, together with the deadening effect of "lining out" may have been responsible for the decline in psalm-singing, which in the eighteenth century degenerated into a dull and lifeless exercise. The principle of individual license in praising God was carried to such an absurd extent that every one claimed the right to sing as he pleased, and the tunes were distorted with all manner of grotesque turns and twists, according to the whim of the singer.

It will be remembered that in the Nonconformist churches organs were not permitted— they were considered an abomination unto the Lord—and there were no trained choirs, conse-

Early psalm tunes.

Decline of psalm singing.

quently the music, such as it was, was confined to unison singing. In the midst of these unpromising conditions came the Wesleyan movement, which for the metrical versions of the Psalms then in use substituted the fervent religious poetry of Charles Wesley and his associates. The hymns were set to the melodies of popular songs and found immediate and widespread acceptance. To "sing like the Methodists" became proverbial, and as in the days of Luther, inspired hymn singing again demonstrated its power over the human soul.

In the meantime the Established Church remained true to Sternhold and Hopkins, but the musical situation was greatly improved by the appearance of Ravenscroft's book of tunes[4] in 1621, an excellent collection of music harmonized in four parts in musicianly manner and with the melody in the tenor part. When Tate and Brady came into vogue Ravenscroft's fine book was superseded by Playford's tunes,[5] a collection arranged in three parts but with the melody in the soprano. These tunes were not

Hymn singing of the Wesleyans.

Hymn singing in the Established Church.

Thomas Ravenscroft (1582?-1635?).

John Playford (1623-1693?).

---

[4] The full title of Ravencroft's Psalter is as follows: "The Whole Booke of Psalmes: With the Hymns Evangelical and spiritual. Composed into 4 parts by Sundry Authors with severall Tunes as have been and are usually sung in England, Scotland, Wales, Germany, Italy, France, and the Netherlands."

[5] The first edition of Playford's Psalter was published in 1671 with the following title: "Psalms and Hymns in solemn musick of four parts on the Common Tunes to the Psalms in Metre: used in Parish Churches." It was, however, a later edition in three parts that became very popular.

comparable with those of Ravenscroft, being of a florid and ornate character.

As to conditions in the early days of this country, church music suffered no improvement when Genevan Psalmody, together with the habit of "lining out," was transferred to New England by the Pilgrims and Puritans. Five tunes, among them Old Hundred, York, and Windsor, comprised the musical stock in trade. The diary of Judge Samuel Sewall, who was for twenty-four years a precentor, throws interesting side-lights on early New England music. The musical sensibilities of the singers were evidently not of a highly developed nature, and there were difficulties regarding the pitch, as no tuning forks or pitch-pipes were in use at the time. The pious and God-fearing Judge chronicles as follows:

> "1705, sixth day, December 28th. Mr. Pemberton prays excellently, and Mr. Willard preaches from Ps. 66:20 very excellently. Spoke to me to set the tune; I intended Windsor and fell into High Dutch, and then, essaying to set another tune, went into a key much too high. So I prayed Mr. White to set it: which he did well, Litchfield tune. The Lord humble me and instruct me, that I should be the occasion of any interruption in the worship of God."

A further note indicates that it was not always the good Judge who was at fault:

"Lord's Day, February 23, 1718. I set York tune, and the congregation went out into St. David's in the very second going over. They did the same three weeks before. This is the second sign. I think they began in the last line of the first going over. This seems to me an intimation and call for me to resign the precentor's place to a better voice."

Early American tunes.

The New Englanders, unlike the Virginians, were not long content with the imported tunes, and with true Yankee enterprise and ingenuity began the manufacture of their own tunes. Among the first to do this was William Billings, who was born in Boston in 1746. His trade was that of a tanner, but his passion was music, and he pursued his self-taught way with great energy and enthusiasm. By this time, through the influence of singing-schools, choirs had come into existence and four-part singing was a possibility. Hymns were gradually coming into use, particularly those of Dr. Watts, and a style of hymn music known as the "fuguing tune" had come over from England. In these tunes, instead of the four parts singing together in the ordinary way, one part would lead off with an animated phrase, which would be imitated in one or more of the remaining parts, somewhat after the style of a fugue. Billings waxes enthusiastic over the fuguing tune and thus describes it:

William Billings.

Fuguing tunes.

"It has twenty times the power of the old

slow tunes, each part straining for mastery and victory, the audience entertained and delighted, their minds surpassingly agitated and extremely fluctuated, sometimes declaring for one part, sometimes for another. Now the solemn bass demands their attention, next the manly tenor: now the lofty counter, now the volatile treble. Now here, now there: now here again,— O ecstatic! Rush on, you sons of harmony!"

Billings' Psalm-books.

Billings was an uncouth but forceful personality and neglected his tanning trade to lead choirs, with a voice that drowned all the others, to publish psalm-books, which had a wide sale, and to compose music, which had a certain crude worth. He succeeded in interesting an influential backing and published successively "The New England Psalm Singer or American Chorister," "The Singing Master's Assistant," "Music in Miniature," "The Psalm-singer's Amusement," "The Suffolk Harmony," and "The Continental Harmony." His tunes became very popular and were sung around the camp-fires of the Revolutionary Army. The best known among them was a tune called CHESTER, and it was frequently played by the fifers in the army.

Oliver Holden and Coronation.

One of Billings' contemporaries and rivals was Oliver Holden, whose tune CORONATION to "All hail the power of Jesus' Name" has quite outlived any effort of Billings' and which is to be found in all the hymn-books of the present generation.

Psalm-singing in New York City.

New England was far more enterprising in matters musical than New York. According to one authority there was as late as the year 1800 practically no Church music in New York City save the Genevan Psalter with its time-worn tunes. The only exception was in Old Trinity Church, Broadway, where we find records of hymn and anthem singing beginning with 1754. Psalm singing was also deeply rooted in our own Church, for we discover that on August 21, 1707, an order was made by the vestry of Trinity parish that the New Version of metrical psalms, by Tate and Brady, shall be introduced "the next Sunday come seven-night, and that no other psalms be sung in ye said church." This would imply that the Old Version of Sternhold and Hopkins had been in use and perhaps with the fine tunes in Ravenscroft's collection (1621).With the advent of Tate and Brady it is likely that Playford's "Whole Book of Psalms" (1677) was drawn upon for tunes, as it was immensely popular in England.

Music at "Old Trinity."

Trinity was supplied with its first organ in 1741. After its installation and following the English custom, the children of the parish charity school were called upon to lead the singing. They were given some instruction in singing, were taught the metrical psalms by rote and a few simple anthems. This was the extent of the music in the parish until the arrival of William Tuckey from England, who advertised himself as "Professor of the Theory and Practise of Vocal Music, late Vicar Choral of the Cathedral Church of Bristol, and Clerk of the parish of St. Mary Port in said city, now resident in New York." He was an indefatigable composer and set about publishing all sorts of hymns, anthems, and services of his own production. He was parish clerk at Trinity for four years, but ceasing to give satisfaction he was dismissed. However, upon the inauguration of a new organ in 1762 his services were secured to organize and drill a mixed chorus, and for the first time a Te Deum was performed in this country. It was announced in the following pompous style in the public press:

William Tuckey.

First performance of a Te Deum.

> "To all lovers of Divine Harmony. Whereas it is the custom in Protestant congregations in Europe on times of rejoicing, as well on Annual as particular days of Thanksgiving, to sing the *Te Deum,* therefore by particular desire, a subscription is opened, for the encouragement of so laudable a practice in this city. Proposals as follows: Every lady, gentleman, etc., to subscribe whatever they please, for which subscription money William Tuckey has obligated himself to teach a sufficient number of persons, to perform the *Te Deum,* either with or without an organ, or other instruments, and that it shall be as good a piece of music

as any of the common *Te Deums* sung in any Cathedral in England."

Up to the beginning of the nineteenth century there is no mention of chanting, but it seems almost incredible with the constantly increasing attention paid to music in Trinity parish that chanting was not attempted. It came eventually, however, for in 1809 a book entitled "The Churchman's Choral Companion to his Prayer Book" was published by Trinity parish, which evidently indicated the musical service at that period. The editor says that "Chants are the only kind of music which is calculated for general use in public worship," and he further remarks that "metre singing, by its fluctuating nature and restless spirit of novelty, is an object of attention to the young and of neglect to the aged." Despite the gradual introduction of anthems, canticles, and services, the hymn singing for years continued to be the psalms in metre. The sectarian churches, however, and particularly the Methodists, were rapidly abandoning the psalms for the hymns of Watts and the two Wesleys.

It is well within the last century that the custom of singing "spiritual songs" or hymns has grown up in the Church of England. While the Church readily took up the Calvinistic habit of metrical psalm-singing it was slow to adopt the hymn-singing of the dissenters. No hymn book met with universal favor or general use until the appearance of "Hymns Ancient and Modern" in 1861, and its success was phenomenal. As to this country, many of us still remember the metrical psalms which were bound up with the Book of Common Prayer in the days when the clergyman would exchange his surplice for an academic gown while preaching the sermon. While "Hymns Ancient and Modern" was used to some extent it was not until 1871, when our own official hymnal was first issued, that psalm-singing was entirely abandoned and hymn-singing in the modern sense of the word became general among us.

Protestant Episcopal Hymnal.

II. CONGREGATIONAL SINGING.

The religious and musical press indulge periodically in heated discussions as to the proper function of music in our church services and the relative importance of the rights of choir and congregation in the matter.

Proper function of music in the church.

Some contend, and with no little asperity, that the worship of Almighty God concerns but the priest on the one hand and the people on the other; that the choir represents the people and the moment anything is sung in which the people can not readily and easily join, the choir usurps the rights of the people and arrogates to itself privileges which it has no authority to exercise. It is "praising God by proxy," a principle which some natures seem incapable of comprehending. These outbreaks are without doubt occasioned by those churches in which the music of the choir is over-emphasized, and where the congregation is deprived of its proper share in the musical portions of the service.

This, however, is a short-sighted view of the situation. If ancient custom and the authority of the primitive Church are to be heeded, the service is divided between three participating bodies, the clergy, the clerks or choristers, and people. The priest is to say or sing the psalms and versicles, to read the lessons, and to join with the clerks and people in the Lord's Prayer, the confession, the psalms and the Creed. The clerks are to join with the people in the responses, the Kyries and the Amens, while the clerks are to sing the anthem, for the rubric says "In quires and places where they sing, here followeth the anthem." According to traditional custom the clerks are also to sing the five anthems in the Communion service: the Nicene Creed, the Sanctus, the Benedictus, the Agnus Dei, and the Gloria in Excelsis.

The people are to take part in the responses, psalms and hymns, but are only to worship negatively while the choir sings the more elaborate music of the service.

The principle of silent worship is obviously as logical as the principle of silent prayer. We

can praise God as effectually through the singing of the choir as we can pray to Him through
the voice of the priest. The *raison d'être* of
congregational singing is the opportunity it
gives both for individual and collective expressions of worship or praise, and the music should
never be of a nature that would debar anyone
from participation on account of its difficulty.
On the other hand, the principle of honoring
Almighty God by dedicating to Him and His
service our noblest architecture, our most beautiful sculpture and painting, and our best diction applies with equal force to our music, and
the special work of the choir should represent
the highest expression of the art and should
be rendered in a manner as far above criticism
as circumstances will permit.

The services of the Church are looked upon
by many people as offering convenient opportunity for the voicing of their personal prayers
and praises. They quite overlook, or fail to
remember, the broader aspect of the case, which
is that these services are also an act of worship
on the part of the Church as a whole, and
contain elements of far greater importance and
dignity than our individual needs or desires.
Thus while the Church makes every provision
for personal approach to and communion
with the Almighty through the use of response
and psalm and hymn, it also has moments when

Advantages of congregational singing.

Worship both personal and general.

the worshipper must forget his personal equation and feel himself a part of the Church Universal. Until this attitude of mind is attained one can never appreciate to the fullest extent the beauty, the force, and the eminent fitness of our liturgy and ritual, and the evident propriety of elaborate and artistic music.

While the choir, then, has its distinct and appropriate place in the economy of our public worship, it would be as inexcusable to have it usurp the functions and rights of the congregation as to have the congregation with its limited musical and artistic capacity attempt to displace the choir in its peculiar province.

Chanting of the Psalter. Confining ourselves to the Book of Common Prayer (for it must be remembered that hymn-singing is not an integral part of our services but an addition thereto), it is in the psalms of David that the people find their chief opportunity of joining in the services of the Church. **Difficulty of chanting.** But most unfortunately the inherent difficulty of chanting, the only practicable way of singing the psalter, is so great that it debars the congregation from active participation. This difficulty in setting prose to music was probably responsible for the versification of the psalms, which adjusted them to popular choral expression. We have already observed how universally these metrical versions were used and how they gradually became replaced by religious poems, commonly called hymns. Among the Scotch Presbyterians and a few other branches of that persuasion, psalm-singing still obtains, but among Christians at large hymn-singing has all but universally superseded psalmody, and has become the one great musical occupation of our modern congregations. Before treating this important subject at length we will consider briefly the other portions of our ritual which present opportunities for congregational singing.

The responses in the choral service are properly the people's part, and the musical setting of Thomas Tallis, written over 300 years ago, has neither been improved upon nor discarded, although occasional sporadic attempts are made to do both the one and the other. Tallis' Responses are simplicity and dignity itself in their original form, but they have undergone a curious perversion. In Tallis' time it was the custom to write the melody in the tenor part, and the alto and soprano were independent parts added above. People nowadays take it for granted that the melody is in the soprano part, and when they hear Tallis' Responses they join in the soprano instead of the tenor part. It would be far better if choirs would adopt the Ferial or daily arrangement of the responses, for in this arrangement the original plainsong melody is put in the soprano part, or better yet

Choral responses.

Tallis' setting.

to have the plainsong sung in unison until it is thoroughly acquired by the congregation. When the custom has been once thoroughly established it would have a fine effect on festivals to have the choir sing the usual Festal arrangement while the people sing their proper part in the plainsong melody.

Harmonized Confessions and Creeds. A reprehensible habit is the custom of using harmonized Confessions and Creeds.[6] These parts, together with the Lord's Prayer, should be so simple that every one can join in, and they should therefore be monotoned or sung to a single tone. The organ may play varied harmonies, but to have the choir sing anything which discourages participation—and in the Confession of all things—is certainly an infringement on the rights of the people and should not be tolerated. The so-called "Ely Confession" is very "nice" from a musical point of view, but is unquestionably wrong in principle. Furthermore, the habit of singing the responses with expression and with exaggerated ritards and diminuendos is a piece of sentimentality that is without warrant. It is not to be expected that a congregation can indulge in the finer nuances of artistic interpretation and the worshippers feel instinctively that their coöperation is out of place. Those who do join in

---

[6] This criticism does not refer to anthem settings of the Nicene Creed in the Communion Service which are not intended for the people.

merely mar the performance of the choir. In the anthems and services the choir has ample opportunity to exhibit its finesse as well as its prowess, and it can well afford to leave to the people their few opportunities of congregational singing.

The practical difficulties of chanting the psalter have been alluded to, but it is quite possible for all to join in the chanting of the canticles, as they are sung so frequently that the pointing is soon fastened in the memory. The singing of the Venite is perhaps as generally joined in by the congregation as the singing of the hymns. Next to this comes the Nunc Dimittis in point of familiarity, and then the Benedictus. The Te Deum, the Magnificat, and Nunc Dimittis are apt to be sung to anthem settings, where they have choirs of ability, and sad to say, too often where they have choirs of so little ability that it would be far better and more edifying to use simple chants. When the canticles are chanted the choirmaster should see to it that the music selected is of a simple and straightforward character and of a nature to invite coöperation on the part of the worshippers.

There are simple anthem settings of the canticles, particularly of the Magnificat and Nunc Dimittis, which are well within the capacity of the congregation. It would be very advantageous if such were printed on card-board slips and distributed among the pews. It would be an indication that all were expected to take part in the performance of the music, and the printed notes would be of assistance to many.

The Gloria in Excelsis. There is one hymn of the ancient Church which next to the long metre doxology is more generally known than any one musical number in our whole liturgy, *i. e.,* the Gloria in Excelsis to the so-called "Old chant." It is a thousand pities that the music is of such an unsatisfactory character. Its source is unknown, but the chant itself is known and sung not only throughout our own Communion but among the various Protestant denominations also. A custom so widespread and long established is almost impossible to supplant, but it is most devoutly to be wished that some day an equally simple but better and worthier musical setting may be found and become universally current.[7]

We will now return to the important subject of hymn-singing.

Hymn singing essentially congregational. Hymn singing is essentially and fundamentally a congregational function. It is equally deplorable whether this function be largely taken over by a trained choir, or whether through general apathy and indifference it de-

---

[7] May that day also include a correction of the text and avoid the redundant appearance of the phrase "that takest away the sins of the world, have mercy upon us," which doubtless crept in through the typographical error of a "printer's doublet."

generates into a lifeless and listless practice. Nothing is more inspiring than good, hearty congregational singing, nothing attracts and holds people so effectually, and nothing creates in so large a measure religious zeal and fervor. The hymn singing of a congregation is almost an unfailing barometer of its spiritual condition. Good hymn singing is a sure indication of a wide awake and energetic parish, one where the people turn out and join sincerely in the service. On the contrary, poor hymn singing is an index of spiritual indifference and stagnation. With such a powerful agency at hand for the promotion of genuine religious feeling and enthusiasm it is singular that hymn singing is not assiduously and systematically cultivated. It is within the means of the humblest parish, for it is not, happily, a question of expense, but of well-directed intelligence, skill, and devotion to the cause.

How shall we secure this desirable custom of hearty and spontaneous hymn singing?

It is a difficult question to answer, for conditions vary in every parish and suggestions that might aid in one case might prove quite futile in another. We can only generalize in the hope that some of the suggestions offered may be found of practical value, or, failing in this, that such an awakening of interest may re-

How to
secure good
hymn
singing.

sult that better methods may be discovered than any hinted at in this lecture.

In the average congregation we have a musically crude but not altogether incapable mass of people. There are comparatively few who absolutely cannot "carry a tune" as the phrase goes. In fact they are in about the same proportion as the color-blind. But many are timid, others indifferent, and the usual result is a faint-hearted attempt at singing by perhaps one-half of the congregation. Take this same body of people, let them attend some public gathering where their patriotic feeling is thoroughly aroused and they will sing *America* in a manner that will leave no doubt as to their vocal possibilities.

This experiment simply establishes the fact that the ability to sing is there provided the incentive is sufficiently strong.

The maxim "to him that hath shall be given" and its converse are most aptly proven by congregational singing. A stranger enters a large church where everybody sings, and sings heartily. He immediately feels encouraged to join in and adds his quota to the inspiring general effect. Per contra, he attends a small church where apathy and listlessness prevail and he hesitates to open his mouth, however much he may wish to do so.

How shall we improve our congregational

singing; how get those who sing to sing better, **Intelligent guidance of clergy necessary.** and how encourage to sing those who do not sing at all? There is only one way and that is by the enthusiasm, the hearty interest and the judicious guidance of the clergy in coöperation with the choirmasters and organists. How often is the importance of singing mentioned in our churches? How often are the people urged to join in more earnestly? What attempts are made to give the people a little instruction or direction in their singing?

To accomplish anything the importance of music must be magnified, interest must be aroused and a desire to do something awakened. When a vested choir is once installed all thought of congregational singing is apt to be forgotten, and no attempt is made to encourage or increase the participation of the people. A **Choir should encourage congregational singing.** choir is not performing one of its most important duties if it does not improve the hymn singing. As a matter of fact it generally does so, but this result is accidental rather than intentional.

Sir John Stainer brought the choir of St. **Sir John Stainer an advocate of congregational singing.** Paul's Cathedral, London, from a state of indifference and incapacity to one of the highest beauty and efficiency. He was equally interested in the people's part of the service and contended that in the ideal church the congregation should form a vast amateur choir. A choir, amateur or otherwise, necessarily implies rehearsing, and herein lies the crux of the whole situation. If our Church people could only be sufficiently interested to attend an occasional rehearsal, wonders would be accomplished. If they could be induced in some way as a body to give a few minutes to instruction and rehearsal at stated intervals, the results would amply repay any effort involved in drawing them together. Why could not a Sunday evening, say once a month, be given over to hymn singing? A shortened form of Evening Prayer might open the service and the remainder of the hour be devoted to informal talks on the history of Church music and the rehearsing of congregational music.[8]

The talks should include information concerning both hymnology and hymn music, for an appreciation of the literary worth of hymns is quite as essential and quite as interesting as the study of the tunes. If widely advertised such a service would tend to attract non-church members as well as non-church goers, for the love of hymn singing is more widespread than the love of church-going. An absolute condition to success would be a liberal supply of hymnals *with the music.*

---

[8] Of course it would be far better to hold these proposed rehearsals on a week night, and in some gathering place other than the church itself, but in these days of endless demands upon one's time the Sunday afternoon or evening would probably be found more favorable.

In this regard we may well learn from our Methodist brethren. A new official Methodist hymnal was put forth about three years ago. It has better music type, better letter press, better paper, better printing and better binding than almost any of our hymnals, and an edition with music, in substantial cloth binding, sells for fifty cents. This enables the average church to put hymnals with music in every pew, and the far-sighted policy that supplies so excellent a book at such a minimum of cost will greatly improve the singing in the Methodist churches. Their congregational singing, too, stands in far less need of improvement than ours. Another point worthy of imitation is that the Methodist Church itself, through its Book Concern, publishes the hymnal, and consequently profits largely from its sales. The low price has resulted in an enormous demand with corresponding profits to the Church at large.[9]

The advantage of a liberal supply of hymnals containing the music lies in the fact that now-a-days so many people have some knowledge of musical notation, and while they may not be ready readers, the sight of the music is a great encouragement and assistance in the learn-

---

[9] It is gratifying to note that this new Methodist Hymnal appropriates many of our best hymns and tunes. It marks a great advance over its predecessor in both literary and musical value.

ing of new tunes. It gives confidence to the singer as well as a feeling of responsibility.

In case a congregation is brought to the point of attending rehearsals it would be an interesting experiment to treat it as a choral society and to divide the singers into the four parts: soprano, alto, tenor, and bass. In any considerable body of people there is sure to be a certain percentage of singers who have had experience in part singing, and a still larger percentage who could carry their respective parts with a little practice. These two elements would soon be sufficiently strong to carry the weaker singers with them and the result would be a properly constituted choral body prepared to sing modern hymns as they should be, *i. e.,* in harmony. Thus instead of having nine-tenths of the people singing the melody—a very unbalanced and unmusical arrangement—the hymns would be sung with properly balanced parts instead of a few singers here and there essaying something besides the soprano part. Also it would heighten the pleasure and interest of the singers to sing and hear sung all the parts of the harmony. The scheme may be considered visionary, but it is an experiment well worth trying where there is a good sized congregation. If the hymn practice met with success, chanting might be attempted and perhaps simple anthem settings to the canticles.

Congregation as choral society.

Another plan to encourage the singing of the congregation is to forego the usual services of the choir in the chancel on occasion and to distribute the choristers throughout the church, so that by their singing they may stimulate more general participation. The music should of course be of a strictly congregational character and familiar to the people. Still another plan would be to have an auxiliary informal choir sit in the front pews or some section of the church where their efforts would be effective.

If none of these suggestions are practicable naught remains but exhortations and urgings on the part of the priest and painstaking care on the part of the choir and organist to make the hymn singing as attractive as possible, with the hope of winning hearty response from the pews.

As to the choice of tunes there is but one thing to do. Use the very best tunes available and ample interest will be returned upon the investment. It is a mistaken notion that good tunes are more difficult to learn than poor tunes; that the congregation will enter more heartily and readily into the singing of trashy tunes than worthy tunes. With the backing of a choir of very moderate attainments it is only a question of slight persistence to establish the custom of singing nothing but thoroughly good tunes, and when this is the case no one will care for anything else. We have such a rich treasury of tunes both ancient and modern that there is not the slightest excuse for lowering our standards or pandering to questionable tastes.

Plainsong tunes.

To start with, the plainsong tunes—those noble melodies which have stood the wear and tear of ages—should be given a fair trial. They are especially suited for congregational use as they should invariably be sung in unison, and they are the only tunes which are quite satisfactory without accompaniment. They speak to us at first with unfamiliar phrases and we are disposed to reject them because they are not "pretty." Prettiness is the last attribute of a good hymn tune. We may have "pretty" waltzes, serenades, or nocturnes, but not pretty hymn tunes. A hymn tune may be graceful, beautiful, attractive, and ear-pleasing, but unless it has a certain undertone of earnestness and reverence it should have no place in the services of the Church. We can in our tunes run the whole gamut of religious emotion from the depths of woe to the most joyous exuberance and still maintain a certain balance of dignity. The plainsong tunes are never trivial or commonplace but are strong and rugged and full of character. Most of us are familiar with "O Come, O Come, Emmanuel" and appreciate its uncompromising straightforwardness. There are six or eight more plainsong tunes in our hymnals and at least "O Quanta Qualia" and "Veni Creator Spiritus" should not be overlooked. They do not follow the agreeable curves of modern melodies, but what they lack in grace they more than atone for in freedom and vigor. If properly sung their unconventionality and unworldliness will finally bring conviction.

Another class of tunes admirably adapted for congregational singing are the sturdy and historic tunes of the German Lutheran Church. They, too, are best sung in unison and the manly vigor of "Now thank we all our God" and the deep pathos of the Passion Chorale, "O sacred Head surrounded," are typical and well-known instances of sterling worth.

German chorales.

The early English composers have also given us most excellent tunes for congregational use, such as Dundee, St. Anne, St. Peter and Tallis' Evening Hymn, and succeeding composers have added to the list. The modern tunes of Dykes and Barnby, while more graceful in outline and more gracious to the ear, are not so well adapted for unison singing, as the melodies lack the strength and solidity necessary when a considerable number of adult male voices are singing the air. It is not contended by any means that their use should be discouraged on this account, but from an artistic or ideal standpoint they are open to criticism when sung in unison. They only obtain their full effect when sung by a good

English tunes.

choir with well-balanced parts. To sensitive ears such tunes as Barnby's MERRIAL to "Now the day is over," or his setting to "O paradise," or Dykes' "Lead, kindly light," have a very clumsy and ill-balanced effect when sung in unison, and this is one of the reasons why musicianly organists sometimes shrug their shoulders or make wry faces when the congregation is singing.

General participation first aim.

We cannot, however, look for over-refinement in congregational singing. The primary question is not one of artistic effect but of devotional uplift through hearty co-operation on the part of the worshippers. If this is attained in any considerable degree we can well dispense with ultra-esthetic considerations, although our constant aim should be to have our musical efforts on as high a plane as possible. It would be well if the hymn-tune composers of the future paid more attention to unison tunes which leave scope for varied treatment in the accompaniment.

Variety in hymn singing.

The possibilities for variety in hymn singing are not usually considered. Aside from the combined forces of choir and congregation we have the following factors:

I. The choir as a whole in harmony.
II. The choir as a whole in unison.
III. The men of the choir in unison.
IV. The boys of the choir in unison.

V. The congregation as a whole.

VI. The men of the congregation alone.

VII. The women of the congregation alone.

VIII. Solo voices singing or in combination.

Take for example the Palm Sunday hymn, St. Theodulph. "All glory, laud, and honor," to the German tune St. Theodulph by Teschner, which is usually sung as a processional. It is rather taxing to sing through consecutively and the following suggestions will relieve the strain and make it far more varied and effective:

Verse I. "All glory, laud, and honor," choir and congregation in harmony.

Verse II. "Thou art the King of Israel," men of choir and congregation in unison.

Verse III. "The company of angels," women and boys in unison.

Verse IV. "The people of the Hebrews," men of choir and congregation in unison.

Verse V. "To Thee before Thy passion," women and boys in unison.

Verse VI. "Thou didst accept their praises," all voices in unison.

The refrain "All glory, laud, and honor" to be sung by all in harmony as far as possible.

It will be observed that there is a certain amount of appropriateness in the distribution of the verses between the low and high voices. Of course such a procedure necessitates either printed or verbal explanations and the sympathetic co-operation of the congregation, but the final effect is worth some pains to secure.

Sarum.

Barnby's fine tune SARUM to "For all the saints" can be made very attractive by distributing the verses after the following programme:

Verse I. All the voices in harmony as far as possible.

Verse II. All the men's voices in unison in the melody.

Verse III. The congregation alone.

Verse IV. Choir alone in harmony.

Verse V. All men in unison.

Verse VI. Choir alone in harmony.

Verse VII. Congregation alone.

Verse VIII. All the voices in unison with free accompaniment.

To have the congregation sing alone is by no means an unheard of thing, as it has been successfully accomplished in a number of churches and with striking effect.

Several of Dykes' picturesque tunes are especially adapted for choir and congregation or solo and congregation, such as "I heard the voice of Jesus say," "Come unto Me ye weary," and "Christian, dost thou see them." "Art thou weary" is also well suited for solo and chorus.

Tempo of tunes.

In regard to the rate of speed in hymn-singing it is impossible to lay down any hard and fast rules. The size of the building, the number of singers, the nature of the occasion, and the character of the tune must all be considered. Young and enthusiastic choirmasters are apt to force the speed at the expense of dignity, but too quick movement is no greater fault than intolerable dragging.[10]

This intolerable dragging obtains largely in Germany and Holland, where it becomes frequently most distressing. The one virtue is the fact that no one attempts to sing anything but the melody, for the organist is apt to play very elaborate and constantly changing harmonies. He plays the melody very prominently and religiously keeps one note ahead of the congregation. The people sing lustily, however, even if they frequently consume nearly two minutes in a four line hymn. To judge from the original notation the chorale melodies were sung in more varied rhythm than is the custom now, and some writers contend that they were taken with much more life and freedom, and thus account for their enormous popularity in Luther's time. This is indeed strange, for one is prone

---

[10] The writer once heard the Litany hymn, *Saviour, When in Dust to Thee*, sung about twice too fast. It was done without accompaniment and with excellent tone quality. In remonstrating with the organist after the service, the latter maintained that if the hymn had been sung more slowly the singers would lose the pitch. Here is a case in point. The congregation was ignored that the choir might be exploited and the character of the hymn was totally destroyed in order that the choir might keep up to the pitch. In both instances the more important principle was sacrificed for the lesser.

to think that the element most admired in the German chorale is its sustained dignity, and to change its stately and even flow would be to destroy its most eminent characteristic.

Best hymn singing in England.

Taken as a whole England probably has the best congregational singing of any country, as she has also the best choirs and the best organs. In no country is the love and practice of choral singing so universal and the Church reaps the benefit of this praiseworthy habit. English traditions, therefore, should not be treated slightingly in regard to the speed rate of hymn tunes, and a noted authority gives the following metronome marks for certain familiar tunes:

(The beat of a metronome is gauged so many beats to the minute.)

St. Anne	66
Old Hundred	80
St. George's, Windsor	92
Aurelia	96
Eventide	100
Ewing	100
Ellers	104
St. Gertrude	104

Some of these marks will doubtless be considered too slow by the impetuous American, whose restless blood clamors for excitement even in the hallowed precincts of the House of God. But those who appreciate dignity and true reverence will find them not far astray.

Certain Church musicians of the more conservative stripe are disposed to set up the German chorale as the one type and standard of hymn tune. They overlook the fact that modern hymns have a more personal and introspective character than those of the Lutheran era and that they require a corresponding musical interpretation. To sing the typical chorale melody to modern religious poetry is an anachronism and a violation of good taste. The early hymns dealt largely with objective expressions of praise, of faith, or of penitence, and the early tunes were of such interpretative amplitude as to do duty for a considerable variety of texts. There were, of course, instances of close association of words and music, but it arose more from custom than any inner bond of connection.

Nowadays we expect a tune to closely fit the sentiment of the words, to enhance their mood and reinforce their meaning. When a tune is found that thoroughly accomplishes this object to the satisfaction of those competent to judge, it is a wise policy to leave it undisturbed. Both text and tune gain by association and the two form a homogeneous whole with which familiarity does not breed contempt. On the contrary, they become more and more beloved with use. Imagine the Christmas season without "Hark! the herald angels sing,"[11] and "O come,

---

[11] The well-known tune to this hymn (originally *Hark! how all the welkin rings*) was adapted from Mendelssohn's *Festgesang* by W. H. Cummings in 1855. According to Mendelssohn's own opinion the tune was not suitable for sacred words.

all ye faithful," or Eastertide without "The strife is o'er" and "Jesus Christ is risen to-day," sung to their familiar tunes, associated as they are with our earliest years! No new tunes, however good or attractive, could awaken the same emotions or mean so much to us! But no rule is without its exception and it does rarely happen that a new tune is better than the old and worthy to displace it. But we must be quite sure of our ground and not be carried away by passing fancies. For example, the hymn "Jerusalem, the golden" to the tune EWING —a thoroughly good and characteristic setting. In some churches this fine tune has been discarded for a jingling melody which begins like "Yankee Doodle" and ends with a shriek on A-flat. The absurd part of the whole matter is that EWING is found fault with for its extreme range while this other tune goes two notes higher![12]

---

[12] Dr. Neale, who so beautifully translated *Jerusalem, the Golden* from the original Rhythm of Bernard of Cluny, thus writes: "I have so often been asked to what tune the words of Bernard may be sung, that I here mention that of Mr. Ewing, the earliest written, the best known, and with children the most popular: no small proof, in my estimation, of the goodness of Church music." The melody originally appeared in triple rhythm, as follows:

The use and choice of tunes should be governed by deeper principles than ephemeral pleasing qualities. Clap-trap effects and cheap construction are as objectionable in music as they are in literature, and a lack of knowledge or taste scarcely justifies their exploitation. If one is inexperienced he need not look far for expert and capable opinion either among men or books. While liberal allowance must be made for individual opinion and taste there is nevertheless a fairly well-defined line where good music ceases and poor music begins.

Choice of tunes should be well considered.

Familiarity with a good tune is precisely analogous to familiarity with a good poem. It is a valuable addition to our spiritual stock-in-trade and something to be appreciated and treasured.

There is a strong feeling for greater unity on the part of nearly all Christian bodies, and a constantly growing bond of sympathy is the use of certain hymns and tunes which have become

Hymns a bond of unity.

well-nigh universal throughout the Christian world. Each new edition of the sectarian hymnals draws more and more from the best Anglican sources. The German chorales are finding their way into the better English and American hymn-books of all denominations. The Roman Catholics do not hesitate to borrow from us and from Protestants generally, not even drawing the line at that war-cry of the Lutherans, *"Ein' Feste Burg ist Unser Gott."*

Accounts are balanced by the growing interest in plainsong music, which had its development largely in the Church of Rome. This interchange of congregational music of all creeds cannot but soften prejudice, increase sympathy, and call attention to much that is common to all Christian believers.

Eclectic spirit necessary.

All schools of hymn music have their place and their peculiar value, and it behooves us of the Anglican Church to cultivate an eclectic spirit that our congregational music may become wide in scope and rich in quality.

III.

The Organan.

There are few evidences of the skill and in- **Organ as an instrument.** genuity of man that can compare with the church or concert organ as it stands to-day. From a purely mechanical point of view it is an extremely complex instrument, its construction calling for a practical knowledge of carpentry and cabinet-making, of pneumatics and hydraulics, of electricity and acoustics, as well as of the handling of metal and leather. On the artistic side it requires furthermore a keen sense of tone color and a feeling for proportion and balance in the distribution of the various qualities of sound. In the exposed portions of the instrument it touches upon the arts of architecture and mural decoration. Without the artistic sense mechanical resourcefulness would count but little, for we admire an organ finally for its beauty of tone and its majestic volume of sound rather than for the cleverness of its action, the ease of manipulation, or the attractiveness of its case.

The origin.

To a person interested in both music and mechanics there are few more fascinating pursuits than the study of the development of this king of instruments. Tradition has it that the wind blowing through a broken reed gave the first suggestion of the organ pipe. In any event, the production of agreeable tones by blowing across the edge of a pipe or reed was probably known in Jubal's time, and his "organ" may have been a number of such pipes bound together, whose graduated lengths gave forth the notes of the scale. An instrument of this sort was known among many ancient peoples. The Greeks, for instance, called it a syrinx, after a lovely water maid beloved by Pan. This instrument was in common use and contained from three to nine pipes, the usual number being seven. While the first pipes were made of reeds they were later made of horn, ivory, bone, wood, or metal.[1]

Greek Syrinx. Pipes of Pan.

As these pipes were closed at the lower end they give the first example of the so-called "stopped pipes" which have the acoustical peculiarity of giving a tone nearly an octave lower than the same length of pipe would produce if left open. In the earliest types the pipes were

---

[1] According to the legend Syrinx did not reciprocate the love of Pan, and to escape his importunities she fled, and was changed by her sisters into a reed. However, this did not lessen Pan's devotion, for he cut the reed and divided it into seven portions, gradually decreasing in size. These he bound together with wax and formed a musical instrument upon which he continued to voice his passion.

stopped by nature, as the reeds were cut off just below the knot.

The Chinese employed twelve or sixteen tubes of bamboo, while the Peruvians made use of both cane-stalks and soapstone in their instruments. Later this "banded-together" series of tubes became known as Pandean Pipes, and they are still to be found in remote sections of Europe where modern civilization has not yet penetrated. These pipes of Pan were quite popular in England a century or so ago with travelling musicians, and they are still occasionally to be met with in connection with Punch and Judy shows. A modern Roumanian specimen in the South Kensington Museum in London contains twenty-five tubes arranged in a curve.

Chinese and Peruvian Pandean pipes.

Modern Roumanian specimen.

In time it was discovered that the tone could be more easily produced by arranging a mouthpiece after the manner of a penny whistle, rather than by the original method of blowing across the top of the tube.

The Egyptians seem to have been the first to discover this principle as well as that of lateral holes in the pipe to govern the length of the column of air, thus securing a series of tones from one pipe.

Egyptian pipes.

As the deeper toned pipes were exhausting to blow by the mouth, the construction of a reservoir or wind-chest followed, upon which the pipes were placed, tightly fitting into holes made to receive them. Wind was supplied by two blowers blowing alternately with their mouths through flexible tubes into a wind-chest. At first all the pipes sounded at once unless silenced by the hand or fingers.[2]

Mechanical progress. The next advance was the placing of slides underneath each pipe, by the manipulation of which the air could be admitted or cut off at will, and the wind supply was greatly improved by replacing the human mouth with a smith's bellows. Pipes were made of various metals as well as of wood, and these crude instruments gradually increased in size and power.

Popular use. By the beginning of the Christian era organs of this type were in common use, and some of them were fitted out with very clever blowing **Hydraulic organs.** devices, the so-called "hydraulic organ" making use of the weight of water to regulate the wind supply. "Open" pipes, "stopped" pipes, and "reed" pipes were in use, thus giving variety of tone quality, and most of the underlying principles of modern organ construction were at least suggested in these rough prototypes. A quotation from the poet Claudian about 400 A. D. refers to the hydraulic system of blowing and indicates that organs were large, powerful,

---

[2]The use of skins as a reservoir for wind, after the manner of a bagpipe, was a device known to the Greeks as early as 400 B. C.

and easy of manipulation in his day. He speaks as follows:

> "Let there be also one who by his light touch forcing out deep murmurs and managing the unnumbered tongues of the field of brazen tubes, can with nimble finger cause a mighty sound; and can move to song the waters stirred to their depths by the massive lever."

Julian the Apostate is said to have referred to an organ of the fourth century in the following terms:

A fourth century organ.

> "I see a strange sort of reeds; they must, methinks, have sprung from no earthly, but from a brazen soil. Wild are they, nor does the breath of man stir them, but a blast, leaping forth from a cavern of ox-hide, passes within, beneath the roots of the polished reeds; while a lordly man, the fingers of whose hands are nimble, stands and touches here and there the concordant stops of pipes: and the stops, as they lightly rise and fall, force out the melody."

St. Jerome is quoted as describing an organ at Jerusalem, with twelve brazen pipes, two elephant skins, and fifteen smith's bellows, which could be heard at the Mount of Olives, a distance of nearly a mile.

A fifth century organ.

The value of the organ for Church purposes was soon perceived, especially as an aid to the singing. It appears that Spain in the fifth century was the first to use the instrument for

Organ in worship.

this purpose, being followed by Italy, England, France, and Germany, in the order named.

A Spanish organ.

A Spanish organ is described in Hawkins' "History of Music" as being two feet long, six inches broad, and furnished with fifteen playing slides and thirty pipes. An organ of such dimensions would be far different in size from the one mentioned by St. Jerome at Jerusalem, but it was probably intended for choir purposes only.

Venice, France, Germany, England.

Venice was noted for its fine organs in the ninth century, but later France and Germany were said to produce the best instruments. About this period organs with pipes of brass or copper became numerous in England. An old manuscript Psalter in the library of Trinity College, Cambridge, contains an interesting picture of a tenth century organ. Eleven pipes varying in length from about three inches to two feet are mounted upon a wind-chest, and four men manipulating as many levers are supplying the wind. Two organists are evidently urging the blowers to greater effort. Two performers for eleven pipes seems a liberal allowance when we consider that nowadays one organist manages several thousand pipes unaided.

Eleventh century treatise on organ building.

A treatise on organ building appears as early as the eleventh century and it describes very fully the construction of instruments at that time. This treatise informs us that a letter was attached to the tongue of each slide in order to indicate the pitch. These slides fitted into slits like the lid of a domino box, and they necessitated double motions as the opening of one slide was accompanied by the simultaneous closing of the one used previously.

The following account of an organ in Winchester Cathedral gives an excellent idea of the development of the organ in England in the tenth century. It is by a monk named Wulstan, who died in 963:

Winchester Cathedral.

> "Such organs as you have built are seen nowhere fabricated on a double ground. Twice six bellows above are ranged in a row, and fourteen lie below. These, by alternate blasts, supply an immense quantity of wind, and are worked by 70 strong men, laboring with their arms, covered with perspiration, each inciting his companions to drive the wind up with all his strength that the full-bosomed box may speak with its four hundred pipes which the hand of the organist governs. Some when closed he opens, others when open he closes, as the individual nature of the varied sound requires. Two brethren (religious) of concordant spirit sit at the instrument, and each manages his own alphabet. There are moreover, hidden holes in the forty tongues, and each has ten pipes in their due order. Some are conducted hither, others thither, each preserving the proper point (or situation) of its own note. They strike the seven differences of joyous sounds, adding the music of the lyric semitone.

Like thunder the iron tones batter the ear, so that it may receive no sound but that alone. To such an amount does it reverberate, echoing in every direction, that every one stops with his hand his gaping ears, being in no wise able to draw near and bear the sound which so many combinations produce. The music is heard throughout the town, and the flying fame thereof is gone out over the whole country."

Great and choir organs. This most interesting account indicates that two organs, corresponding to our Great and Choir organs, were in use, that to increase the volume ten pipes were in operation with each slide, and that each player "managed his own alphabet," or in other words, manipulated the tongues with their appropriate letterings.[3] The three sets of playing slides doubtless controlled different degrees of force, so that a limited degree of variety was possible.

Magdeburg Cathedral First key-board. In the eleventh century at the Cathedral in Magdeburg we hear for the first time of an organ with a key-board. It is said to have contained sixteen notes, but the keys were far different from the narrow strips of ivory of to-day. These first efforts consisted of a key, or more properly a lever, from three to five inches in width, and the action was so stiff that it required a blow from the fist to operate it. Hence, organists were first called "organ beaters." The

---

[3] The "seven differences of joyous sounds" refers to the seven notes of our C major scale, the "lyric semitone" being B flat, the first chromatic note to be introduced into the scale.

addition of the sharps or flats was a process of slow evolution. The "lyric semitone" B flat was added about the tenth century. This was followed in order by F sharp, E flat and G sharp. It was probably the fourteenth century before all twelve notes of the chromatic scale were in use. At first these additional notes were played from shorter levers, separated from and above the original keys—almost like another key-board. The long and short keys were later brought close together and reduced in size so that they could be played by alternating the thumb with the fingers. This process of reduction in size was gradually continued until the present dimensions were reached. *[Introduction of sharps and flats.]*

By the fourteenth century churches were very generally supplied with organs and they were of two sorts, positive or stationary organs, and portative or movable organs. The portative, or regal organs, as they were also called, were so small that they could readily be moved from place to place and they were used to accompany the plainsong of the choir. *[Positive and portative organs.]* The positive organ of Halberstadt Cathedral, built in 1361 by Nicholas Faber, a priest, was the most famous instrument of its day. It contained three claviers or key-boards, twenty-two keys, fourteen of which were diatonic and eight chromatic, the wind being supplied by twenty bellows blown by ten men. Its largest pipe was *[Halberstadt Cathedral. Nicholas Faber (1361).]*

thirty-one feet in length, approximating in size those of the great instruments of to-day. This organ was so arranged that a portion of the pipes could be silenced at will, thus giving relief to the constant full organ effect which had obtained previously.

Pedal key-board. The introduction of pedals, a key-board for the feet, occurred in the fifteenth century. At first they consisted of one octave only, without chromatics, and their use was confined to long sustained tones, from which custom the present harmonic device of an organ point or pedal point was derived. About this time the four fundamental qualities of organ tone were evolved, the "diapasons," the "flutes," the "strings" and the "reeds."

Development of stop control. The greatest advance, and the one which opened the way for the future development of the organ, was the device whereby any set of pipes could be used at will. In the earlier organs increase of power was gained by adding more pipes to each key. As these pipes were all served by one pallet, they all sounded at once when the pallet was opened by pressure of the key. By the addition of other key-boards with a different selection of pipes a contrast of tone and power was possible, but only in a very restricted way. The first step in advance was a contrivance by which certain of the sets of pipes could be silenced at will. This was followed by the introduction of a long transverse slider which brought into play or silenced any desired set of pipes. The fact that the tone was "stopped" or silenced by this device undoubtedly gave rise to the term "stop" as applied to the handle which adjusted the slider, and the same word also became a collective term for any one set of pipes. For instance, "Flute stop" refers properly to the knob or handle which brings the flute pipes into action, and it also applies to the same set of pipes as a whole.

Although the device of "stopping" pipes originated in Germany it was soon introduced into England. A builder by the name of Antony Dudyngton erected an organ in the church of All Hallows, Barking, near the Tower of London in the year 1519, and it contained three "stops." It was described as a "pair of organs" and had a compass of four octaves, beginning with the note two octaves below middle C. The lowest octave was a so-called "short octave," the keys from C to E flat inclusive being wanting at the lower end. To offset this, the lowest key E sounded the low C, the F sharp key sounded D, and the G sharp key sounded the low E. The remaining keys spoke their proper tones. There was no pedal key-board, as pedals were not added to English organs until some two hundred and fifty years later, although they had been in use on German organs considerably prior to this period.

York Minster organ.

In 1634 York Minster was supplied with a two-manual, or two key-board organ, the Great organ containing nine stops and the Choir organ five. The stops were diapasons, principals, and flutes.

Disorders of the Commonwealth.

At this period the progress of organ building in England, together with that of music and the arts in general, received a severe blow due to the religious and political upheavals of the Commonwealth. In 1643 it was ordained by Parliament "that all organs and the frames and cases wherein they stand in all churches and chapels aforesaid shall be taken away and utterly defaced, and none other hereafter set up in their places." In the following year a second ordinance "for the further demolishing of monuments of Idolatry and Superstition" was enacted. In pursuance of these orders many organs were completely destroyed. At Westminster Abbey we are told the "soldiers brake down the organs and pawned the pipes at several ale houses for pots of ale." Luckily a number of the prominent Cathedral organs escaped as well as certain in the principal colleges of Oxford and Cambridge.

The puritanical prejudice against musical instruments compelled organ builders to turn to other trades. By the time of the Restoration there were few who had retained their cunning. Bernard Schmidt, a noted organ maker, was induced to come to England from Germany. He soon attained to such fame and popularity that he was known far and wide as "Father Smith." He and his rival, Renatus Harris, were the first great organ builders of England. Remnants of their skilled workmanship in the way of pipes and organ cases may be found to-day in some of the most noted English organs. In Father Smith's first organ, built in 1660 in the Banqueting Room, Whitehall, London, he introduced the first "reed" stops in the country, including two Trumpets and a Vox Humana. The Tremolo, or "shaking stop" as it was first called, had already been in use for some fifty years. Another novelty for which Father Smith was responsible was the first "Echo" organ, which contained four stops.[4]

In May, 1664, both Father Smith and Renatus Harris placed organs on trial in the famous Temple Church, London. After a thorough test of nearly two years' duration Father Smith triumphed, but not to the detriment of Harris' reputation.

In 1710 Renatus Harris built in Salisbury

----

[4] The stops in the Echo organ were duplications of certain stops in the Great organ, but they were enclosed in a separate box which muffled the sound and gave the effect of an echo. This was the precursor of the swell organ, which later had the box supplied with movable shutters, making it possible to "swell" or increase the tone.

Cathedral the first four-manual organ in England. The usual Great, Choir, and Echo organs were supplemented by a second Great organ the pipes of which were borrowed from the first Great organ. The first "Swell" organ appeared six years later, the pipes of which were enclosed in a large box. By means of overlapping shutters controlled by a movement of the foot the tone could be varied in volume to a considerable extent. The first "Dulciana" or string-tone stop was brought into England in 1754 by a German named Snetzler. In 1790 the pedal key-board was introduced into England after having been in use in Germany for upwards of four hundred years. In 1809 combination pedals (iron levers, operated by the foot and controlling certain groups of stops) were first applied.

Organs at this period had no definite range. Some had G as the lowest note, some F, and some C. The pedal-board extended two octaves but was not continuous. The upper octave repeated the notes of the lower octave. Many of the stops were incomplete, not extending the whole length of the key-board. The action in the larger organs was very stiff and precluded any rapid passage work. The organist of the celebrated organ at Haarlem, in Holland, was in the habit of stripping like a blacksmith for his arduous hour's work when giving a performance. The necessity for lightening the touch resulted in the pneumatic lever, an invention whereby the finger was relieved from making direct connection between key and pipe. In the pneumatic action the depression of the key admitted wind into a little bellows the inflation of which was utilized as the motive power. This mechanical device was of the greatest importance in the evolution of organ building, as it was now possible to increase their size and scope to any desired extent. The device was invented in 1832 by an Englishman named Barker, but it was first applied practically by the great French organ builder, Cavaillé-Col, in an instrument erected by him in 1841 in the Abbey Church of Saint Denis, near Paris.

Pneumatic action.

Charles S. Barker (1806-?).

In the development of new tone qualities and also in mechanical improvements, the continental builders were considerably in advance of the English.

Influence of continental builders.

At the great Industrial Exhibition of 1851 in Hyde Park, London, a French organ by Ducroquet of twenty stops, and a German organ by Schultze & Sons of fifteen stops, were installed. They both had two manuals and pedal, the French organ having a manual compass of five octaves, the German of four and a half. Pedals and manuals began with C on both organs. These organs attracted much attention owing to the superiority of their tone quality

Ducroquet. Schultze & Sons.

and their general effectiveness, quite eclipsing
the native organs of the same or even larger
size.   Up to this period the tonal appointment
of English organs consisted of diapasons of various pitch and force, and reeds not conspicuous
for their beauty or smoothness.   The French
organ was noticeable for its fine reeds (which
were mounted on a separate sound-board and
supplied with extra wind-pressure), and its
flutes.   The Oboe, Cor Anglais, and Flute were
all excellent imitations of these respective orchestral instruments.   The German organ attracted attention more particularly to its string-
tones stops, having a Gamba and two Geigen
Principals or Violin Diapasons.   The soft-
toned Dulciana up to this time had been the
only string-toned stop known in England, and
that, too, was an importation from Germany, as
has already been mentioned.   These two organs
did much to broaden the horizon of English
builders and a consistent and constant improvement in their output has followed, placing them,
in some respects at least, as the leading exponents of organ building in the world to-day.

To have heard the great Willis organ in St.
Paul's Cathedral, the magnificent instrument
by Hill & Son in Westminster Abbey, the fa-
mous product of Norman & Beard in Norwich
Cathedral, the beautiful instruments by T. C.
Walker & Co. in Southwark Cathedral, and

Walker & Sons in St. Margaret's, Westminster (the latter built to specifications by E. H. Lemare, the noted virtuoso), or the much-talked-of organ by that modern genius, Hope-Jones, in Worcester Cathedral, is to admit that no other country could possibly duplicate so many masterpieces of organ construction by so many different builders.   In France the great house of Cavaillé-Col has erected instruments of the first rank in the Cathedral of Notre Dame, in St. Sulpice and the Madeleine in Paris, and in the Town Halls of Manchester and Sheffield in England, while the house of Merklin has constructed excellent organs.   Germany has lost rank somewhat in recent years and at present has no organ builders of international reputation.   Some of its most famous cathedrals have but inferior instruments, and its reputation for fine organs still rests upon the products of a century or so ago.   Among these are the noted organ built for the monks at Weingarten by Gabler in 1750, the fine Silbermann organ in the Strasburg Cathedral, the Walcker organ in Ulm Cathedral built in 1853, and the Mooser organ in Freiburg, Switzerland, built in 1834. The most famous continental organ is doubtless that at Haarlem, Holland.   This renowned instrument by Christian Müller, was begun in 1735 and was more than three years in building.   It contains sixty stops and is more notable

The great French organs.

The great German organs.

The Haarlem organ.

for its volume and power than for the beauty of its solo stops. It is practically in its original condition to-day as no attempt has been made to modernize it, but it still excites the wonder and admiration of tourists.

Canada:
Casavant
Bros.To turn to America, Canada has produced a firm of organ builders, Casavant Bros. of St. Hyacinthe, Quebec, who are placed in the front rank by the most eminent organists such as Frederick Archer, Clarence Eddy, and E. H. Lemare. In Montreal, Toronto, and other Canadian cities they have magnificent instruments equipped with the most approved modern appliances.

First organ
in America.The first pipe organ in America was imported from England and was the property of Thomas Brattle, treasurer of Harvard College. On his death in 1713 he left it to the Brattle Square Church. This was in the Puritan days when the music consisted of psalm-singing, and instruments were considered too profane to be used in church. The gift was not accepted, as they "did not think it proper to use said organ in the public worship of God." In accordance with the will it was transferred to King's Chapel, Boston, the Episcopalians having no scruples about accepting it. The organ was a small affair of six stops and it is still in existence. Several other organs were brought over from England from time to time, the largest being a thirteen-stop instrument intended as a gift by Bishop Berkeley for the town named after him. As the gift was refused it went to Trinity Church, Newport, R. I.

Probably the first organ builder in America was John Clemm of Philadelphia, who came to this country in 1736. He was born in Dresden in 1690 and learned his art with the famous Andreas Silbermann, the greatest of Germany's organ builders. Clemm was evidently a capable workman, for he was engaged by the vestry of Trinity parish, New York, to build a three-manual organ for their use in 1739. The organ was set up in 1741 and contained ten stops on the Great, ten on the Choir, and six on the Swell, a large instrument for those days. We read that it had a "frontispiece of gilt pipes, and was otherwise neatly adorned." It is probable that many of the stops did not run through and that the Swell manual was of short compass.

First American organ builder. John Clemm (1690-?).

A few years later Edward Bromfield built an organ for a Boston church which is said to have been superior in construction to the imported specimens.

Edward Bromfield.

As old Trinity, New York, has always been in the lead in Church music, the successive organs in that historic church give us a general idea of the progress of organ building in this country. Clemm's organ was evidently not an unqualified success, for after twenty years' use

Organs in "Old Trinity," New York.

John Snetzler.

it was condemned. In 1764 an organ by Snetzler, a German builder, who introduced the Dulciana stop into England, and who built several fine instruments for that country, was imported. This organ was destroyed by fire in 1776 and no description of it remains. In 1791, after the rebuilding of the church, an organ described by the rector as "of no great power, but sweet-toned and well adapted for the size of the building," was brought from England, built by Holland. It had seven stops on the Great, six on the Choir, and six on the Swell, the latter being short one octave at the bass end. It was a "G" organ (having GG as the lowest note), and no pedals. Dr. Edward Hodges, the celebrated English organist, who did so much to make the music of Trinity famous, evidently did not agree with the rector's estimate and spoke of it as "an exceeding poor affair." But such as it was it did

Henry Erben.

duty for forty-five years. In 1846 a new organ, after specifications by Dr. Hodges, was installed by Henry Erben, of New York City, the leading builder of his day, and the instrument still stands as a fine specimen of the art of organ-building. It had several curious features, for it was planned before there was any general consensus of opinion regarding the compass of key-boards and pedals. The Great organ contained twelve stops and extended five and one-half octaves, beginning an octave lower than is the custom now. The Choir organ had sixteen stops and the same compass as the Great, but the lowest octave did not speak. The Swell organ of nine stops had six and one-half octaves, but the lower two octaves were silent except with two stops designed to furnish a deep bass. The organ was supplied with a pedal key-board of two octaves but only one stop, and that of the unusual 32-foot pitch. The lowest pipe is large enough to hold twenty men and fourteen boys. This largeness of scale holds good throughout the organ and gives to it a nobility and amplitude of tone which is lacking in many modern organs even of much larger stop capacity. The roominess of its location and the fine acoustics of the building are also important factors in the satisfying general result.

Jardine & Son of New York City made excellent instruments at this period, not only in this country but also in England. The next firm of note was Hook & Hastings, who for many years held the lead. In 1853 they erected the first large concert organ in Tremont Temple, Boston, which was equipped with four manuals and pedal, seventy stops and nearly 4,000 pipes. Some twenty-five years later they installed a fine instrument in the Cincinnati Music Hall. Their church organs are also famous and are to be found in many of the principal cities of the country.

Boston Music Hall organ.

The art of organ building in this country received a great impetus upon the erection of the great organ in Boston Music Hall in 1863 by Walcker of Ludwigsburg, Germany. It cost $70,000 and was opened with much pomp and ceremony and it became the mecca of all lovers of organ music in America. When the Boston Symphony Orchestra was founded it was discovered that the famous organ interfered with the acoustics of the hall. The decision to remove it in 1884 was received with bitter opposition. The instrument was stored away and finally sold for $1,500.

Rapid Progress.

The development of organ building in recent years in the United States has proceeded at such a rapid rate that it is impossible to more than hint at its progress and expansion. Hook & Hastings had a formidable rival in Johnson of Westfield, Mass., who built many fine church organs, Chicago claiming some forty of them.

Johnson and Son.

Hilborne L. Roosevelt.

Hilborne L. Roosevelt of New York City, a man of ample means and with a passion for organ building, came next to the fore. About thirty-five years ago he entered into the business of organ building with the laudable intention of turning out nothing but the highest class of work regardless of expense. He declined to enter into competition with other firms and asked at least fifty per cent more for his organs than other builders.   He perfected a new wind-chest as well as a tubular pneumatic system, and at the Centennial Exposition at Philadelphia in 1876, he exhibited the first organ with electric action.   His independence, inventive ingenuity, and artistic skill (for the voicing of his pipes received as great attention as the construction of the mechanical parts) set new standards and had a most stimulating effect upon the trade at large.   For a number of years he secured the most important contracts and was an acknowledged leader.   He died in the midst of his ambitions and labors and the business was taken over for a time by his brother Frank.   Later it passed into the hands of the Votey Co. of Detroit, who built the great organ at the World's Fair, Chicago, in 1893.[5]   Roosevelt's principal rival was the Hutchings Co. of Boston, a firm noted for their beautiful and refined organs. The Votey Co. and the Hutchings Co. joined hands about 1901 and at once assumed a pre-eminent position in the organ-building world; constructing organs which embrace the excellencies of the Roosevelt, the Votey, and the Hutchings systems.   A typical and perhaps the best product of the Hutchings-Votey Co. is the magnificent organ in Woolsey Hall at Yale Uni-

First organ with electric action.

Frank Roosevelt.

Votey Co.

Hutchings Co.

Hutchings-Votey Co.

---

[5] This organ is now at Ann Arbor, Mich. in one of the halls of the State University.

Organ at Yale.

versity, built in 1902. It contains four manuals, seventy-eight speaking stops, twenty couplers and all the wealth of modern appliances for mechanical control in the way of pistons and combination pedals.

Austin Co.

Another fine specimen of American organ building is the superb organ by the Austin Organ Co. of Hartford, Conn., in All Saints' Cathedral at Albany, N. Y. Of the more recent organs erected in this country the most notable is the great organ in the College of the City of New York, built by the Ernest M. Skinner Co. of Boston. It represents the culmination of American organ building to date, and it vies with the best English makes in breadth and dignity and the best French makes in brilliancy. As it is intended purely for concert purposes it has been made as orchestral as possible and with remarkable success. Like all great organ builders, Mr. Skinner's genius is equally divided between great mechanical skill and ingenuity on the one hand, and the ability to produce tones of great perfection and beauty on the other.

E. M. Skinner Co.

Robert Hope-Jones.

Any record of organ building either in America or England, however fragmentary, should include mention of the products of the fertile brain of Robert Hope-Jones. Mr. Hope-Jones has invented new qualities of tone color and has introduced radical changes into all departments of organ construction. His latest instruments are so arranged that any stop can be played at any pitch from any key-board. He employs cement swell-boxes with tone reflectors and laminated lead shutters. Instead of draw stops he employs what might be termed an extra key-board, each note of which represents a stop and is thrown on or off by a slight motion of the finger. A clever device automatically provides a "suitable bass" for any combination of stops. A so-called "double-touch" permits the player, by pressing the keys more deeply, to bring additional force to such note or notes as he may desire. Mr. Hope-Jones' abilities attracted wide attention in England before he came to this country. He is now located at Elmira, N. Y., where he is president of the Hope-Jones Organ Co. The organ in the auditorium at Ocean Grove, N. J. (a building seating ten thousand people), exemplifies the Hope-Jones theory of producing unlimited power and considerable variety from comparatively few stops by virtue of his system of pipe construction, voicing, and heavy wind-pressures.

Of Western firms the more prominent are the W. W. Kimball Co., Lyon & Healy, both of Chicago, and the Marshall Bennett Co. of Rock Island, Ill. All these concerns have demonstrated their ability to construct fine organs and have excellent and notable instruments to their

Organ at Ocean Grove.

W. W. Kimball Co. Lyon & Healy. Marshall Bennett Co.

credit.   Lyon & Healy have since ceased the manufacture of organs.

The largest organs in the world are not in churches or cathedrals but in concert halls, and America has the distinction of heading the list. The largest instrument ever constructed was at the Louisiana Purchase Exposition at St. Louis in 1904.   It contained five manuals and pedals, one hundred and forty speaking stops, ninety-nine mechanical appliances, and over ten thousand pipes.   It was built by the Los Angeles Art Organ Co. and its cost is reported to have been one hundred thousand dollars.   The organ was intended for the Convention Hall at Kansas City, Mo., but owing to financial complications it was never erected there, and it has been dismantled since the exposition.   The next concert organs in size are the famous instruments at the Town Hall [6] in Sydney, N. S. W., and at the Royal Albert Hall in London, England. Both these organs are London products, the former by Hill & Son in 1889, and the latter by Willis in 1876.   The fourth largest is in our own city of Chicago in the Auditorium and has four manuals and pedals, with one hundred and seven stops.   It was built by Hilborne L. Roosevelt.

---

[6] This organ has a 64 ft. reed stop on the pedal organ, the largest set of pipes ever constructed.   The lowest tone vibrates but eight times per second.

Largest of all organs in America.

Louisiana Purchase Exposition organ.

Town Hall, Sydney, N. S. W. Royal Albert Hall, London.

Auditorium, Chicago.

The two largest church organs in the world are both in Russia, one at Libau with one hundred and thirty-one stops and the other at Riga with one hundred and twenty-four. The third is in the Cathedral of the Incarnation at Garden City, L. I., and has one hundred and fifteen stops. This instrument marks a new era in organ construction, as it has an electric action the use of which permitted the distribution of the organ in various parts of the church.[7] St. Bartholomew's, New York City, is the sixth in size and numbers ninety-eight stops. This is in reality two organs played from one keyboard, one being in the chancel, the other in the gallery.[8]

Our own Church in this country unquestionably leads in its appreciation of fine organs, and it can take a justifiable pride in the fact that it possesses such a large percentage of the best instruments. That the interest in organs and organ building is widespread is evidenced by the fact that out of the twelve largest organs in the

---

[7] The development of the electric action has made the "Echo organ" possible, whereby a few stops of a more or less "celestial" character are put in some remote place.

[8] In the old days of quartette choirs both singers and organ were placed in the gallery over the main entrance. With the introduction of male vested choirs a chancel organ became necessary. In some churches, notably at "Old Trinity," New York, two organists were employed after the manner of the large churches in Paris, one at the chancel organ to accompany the choir, the other at the gallery organ to play the voluntaries. Several New York churches have had the two organs connected by electricity and played from a combined console in the chancel. The effect of the two organs, especially in hymn-singing, is very fine.

world, America has four. Two of these are in Episcopal Churches, the remaining two being concert organs.

Organ most effective as a church instrument. While as a concert instrument the organ fills a large and important place, it is in the Church that it finds its true sphere of usefulness and effectiveness. Its only rival is the full orchestra, and this, while excelling in brilliancy, facility, and pliancy is lacking in that sustained dignity and serenity which so admirably adapts the organ for the worship of Almighty God. Then it has the practical advantage that it is under the control of one man, and even the most extravagant salary of an organist is but a small matter compared with the maintenance of an orchestra.

Sustained quality aids congregational singing. The sustained quality of the organ tone is especially adapted for the support and encouragement of congregational singing, and this fact alone is of sufficient importance to make the purchase and proper installation of an organ the subject of most earnest thought. Yet the church architect will rarely give the placing of the organ serious consideration, and the average organ committee is concerned mostly about obtaining the greatest number of pipes for the smallest amount of money.[9]

---

[9] The custom which prevails both in this country and in England of placing the selection of an organ in the hands of a committee who have not the slightest technical knowledge, is certainly open to criticism. In Continental Europe the choice of an organ builder in important instances is

We will now consider the practical details involved in the selection of an organ. In the first place it should be selected for its especial place and purpose, being neither too large nor too small, and should be of the very best quality. If funds are not available at once it would be far wiser to build part of a good organ, trusting to its completion some later day, than to rush ahead and install a complete instrument of inferior make.

It is as essential to have an organ placed in a favorable position as it is to have the pulpit, if the instrument is to be heard at its full and proper value. Such a foolhardy experiment as placing the preacher in an inaccessible corner, where his voice would be expected to turn corners, dodge pillars, and penetrate partitions would hardly be attempted, but this is precisely what happens to many a fine instrument.

An English authority, Somers Clark, has the following illuminating suggestions as to the position of the organ:

> "We all know that an organ must have plenty of height above it, space about it, and must not in itself be crowded; but there are other points upon which the opinion of experts would be of value.
>
> "One of these is the position of the key-

---

placed in the hands of organists and musicians of the first rank. For example, when a new organ was required for Notre Dame, in Paris, such men as Auber, Rossini, and Ambroise Thomas headed a committee of specialists.

board in regard to the organ and the choir. Custom, ruled to a great extent by expense, makes it usual to place the organ on one side of the chancel and the organist close to the organ. The organist cannot hear his choir clearly. The half of the choir nearest him sings away from him, the other half sings towards him but has the other mentioned half intervening. He is generally so near the organ that he cannot clearly hear how much or little noise he is making (and my experience is that to be on the safe side he makes too much) and lastly, having the organ and voices so close at hand he knows but little what the congregation is about. As far as the choir is concerned the rules for ample space, height, and width are as essential for the welfare of the voices as of the organ.

"What would then be the conditions of an ideal position for the organist?

"1. That he should hear the choir well.

"2. That he should hear the organ.

"3. That he should be able to see the choir well and also see the clergy who may be serving at the altar.

"4. That he hear the congregation at least fairly well.

"5. That he should have a tolerable sight of the nave of the church and thus be able to keep his eye on processions and other functions taking place there.

"6. We might add that he should be able to see the organ in connection with a side chapel."

G. A. Audsley, in his monumental work on

the *Art of Organ-building,* gives the following rules for a proper placing of the organ:

"1. Sufficient floor space to allow the organ to stand without the slightest crowding—also back and sides to give free egress to sound and easy access to all parts.

"2. Ample height at most favorable elevation, having considerable space above for free emission of sound from all parts.

"3. Arches, large as possible and up to full height of ceiling, the latter to follow shape of the arch.

"4. Every precaution against dampness and to secure equable temperature. External walls should be double and with air space. No windows. Chambers to be lined with narrow grooved and tongued pine, tightly joined, securely nailed and varnished."

Of still greater importance than the disposition of the organ is the selection of the builder, for a location conforming to the ideals of both Mr. Clark and Mr. Audsley will not make a poor instrument sound well. Owing to the general lack of information regarding organ building, even among professional organists, and the complicated mechanism involved, it is a simple matter for an unscrupulous dealer to market a very inferior product. A large number of organ builders look upon their business from a commercial point of view, and either ignore or are ignorant of the fact that good organ building is an art and not a trade. They honestly think

Importance of the selection of a builder.

they have done their whole duty if they have delivered an instrument reasonably well made and conforming outwardly to the specifications. So much pressure is brought to bear upon them through competition and through almost universal efforts to beat them down on their prices by the churches themselves, that they are not altogether to be blamed in the matter.

Organ builders may be classed under three headings:

Unprincipled. builders.

1. The unprincipled builders who deliberately quote a price at which it is impossible to build a good instrument. They are smooth talkers and the uninformed organ committee is easily deceived by their representations. More stops and more pipes are offered than by any reputable maker. Great stress is laid on unimportant details while the essential requisites are carefully avoided. They have large factories and do an extensive business, but almost entirely in small towns or among poor churches. No organist of integrity and standing will endorse them, though some musicians are venal enough to do so for a consideration. What are the results? An instrument is delivered that seemingly complies with a specification not overburdened with details. The mechanical construction is of the cheapest and will constantly cause either expense or annoyance. The organist will rarely have the combined resources of the instrument

at his command, poor as they are. Something will always be out of order. The tone will be harsh and unmusical or weak and characterless; the wind supply is apt to be insufficient; there will be no agreeable variety of tone qualities. The lowest octave of pipes (which in a properly constructed organ will cost as much as the remaining four octaves) will be thin and wheezy, and stopped pipes are likely to be substituted for open ones at a great saving in expense. Even if the congregation is content with such a wretched instrument, no self-respecting organist will play it except under stress of dire necessity. He will always be discontented and always be on the lookout for a better instrument.

2. The second class of organ builders are **Commercial builders.** those who do excellent mechanical work, who are apt to be honest and reliable in their dealings and try to give value received. They are, however, lacking in the artistic sense and in the scientific knowledge necessary for first-class work. One is reasonably sure of obtaining a reliable and durable instrument, of ample volume and considerable variety of tone. Its mechanical features may be excellent, but it will lack the qualities that arouse admiration and provoke enthusiasm, and it will never be a source of especial pride to its owners. It will, however, give good service, and it is this class of organ

that is most frequently to be met with in our well-to-do churches.

3. The third class of organ builders are those who are not possessed alone of mechanical ingenuity and skill, but are also keenly alive to the artistic qualities necessary to produce a really fine instrument. They realize that the foundation of a good organ are the diapasons, that they must be of ample scale and of the best material, yielding nobility of tone with ample body. Furthermore the flutes must be mellow and clear, the strings must have the characteristic "biting" quality and the reeds be pungent and pervading, without coarseness or roughness. To produce work of this quality requires artisans with special gifts for voicing and regulating and the use of the best materials regardless of cost. The best builders take into consideration the size and shape of the building and the location of the instrument. The specifications give regard to the proper grading and grouping of tone values, giving volume on the one hand and delicacy on the other. Ample wind is supplied and every precaution taken to offset the changes of temperature and the effect of dampness.

Organ builders of this class, despite the fact that they will not enter into competition concerning the price, do not amass wealth. On the contrary, they frequently meet with financial reverses or die with but a small share of this world's goods. One of the most noted of English organ builders, who built a large number of the most famous instruments within the last half-century, died recently and left his heirs but a few hundred pounds as the net results of his pre-eminent skill and incessant labor. A builder mentioned earlier in these pages as a man of wealth sank thousands of dollars annually in his laudable desire to do nothing but the highest grade of work. The most prominent organ building firm in the country has recently been forced to make an assignment, and one of the largest music houses in the world, with ample capital, gave up the unequal struggle in trying to make good organs and a reasonable profit at the same time.

The building of a large organ is a matter of such detail and complexity that the final cost to the builder can never be accurately estimated in advance. Unlooked for difficulties in erection, delays in transportation, fluctuation in the price of materials, and labor troubles are among the doubtful factors to be reckoned with. The estimated profit is frequently seriously lessened if not entirely wiped out, when the builder tries honestly to fulfil his contract. To meet the bids of less scrupulous builders would be suicidal, and a price must be asked which seems to the uninitiated decidedly extravagant.

Hints regarding purchase of organ.

A church contemplating the purchase of a new organ would do well to look thoroughly into the matter before deciding to let a contract, and a few hints will be given that may prove of value to those who have no technical knowledge of organ construction. We will take it for granted that the best woods are to be used, thoroughly seasoned, and that the metal pipes will have the proper proportions of tin and zinc. The next matter for consideration is the selection of the stops. Stops, or sets of pipes, are technically named from their tone quality and from their pitch. Stops which **Open pipes.** sound the same pitch as the corresponding notes of the piano are known as "eight-foot" stops because the lowest tone (CC) is produced by an open pipe eight feet in length. As the notes ascend the pipes gradually decrease in length, the next C being one-half the length of the lowest pipe, or four feet, the next C being but two feet in length, and the highest C, three octaves higher, but three inches in length. Piano pitch may also be produced by taking a 4-foot pipe for the lowest tone instead of an **Stopped pipes.** 8-foot, and plugging or stopping the top end of it. This produces an 8-foot tone from a 4-foot pipe, which, however, is dull and lifeless. Open pipes are therefore much more expensive than stopped pipes, as they are twice as large. There are also 4-foot stops which sound an octave higher than piano pitch, 2-foot stops which sound two octaves higher than piano pitch, and 16-foot stops which sound an octave lower. Eight-foot stops are the normal and most important stops for the key-board, while 16-foot stops are the normal and most important stops for the pedal key-board. The conclusion drawn from this perhaps confusing explanation, is that open stops and stops of eight and sixteen foot pitch are the most essential and the most expensive stops of the organ. Cheap builders will load up a specification with stopped pipes and pipes of 4-foot and 2-foot pitch, which will make a great showing of pipes, but their undue proportion results in thinness and shrillness of tone. Mix- **Mixtures.** tures should also be looked upon with suspicion in small organs, for they are not needed. They swell the total number of pipes, as three or more pipes are used to each note, but they are exceedingly small. Mixtures have, however, an important place in large organs, adding a rich and "crashy" effect to the full organ. The cheap builder will also lessen his expense considerably by using poor material and by reducing the scale or dimensions of the pipes at the expense of the tone quality. The open diapasons when **Scales too** of ample scale, and properly constructed reed **small.** stops, such as the Oboe, Cornopean, Clarinet, Trumpet, Vox Humana, etc., represent the greatest items of expense as far as the stops are concerned, but upon their quality depends the real worth of the organ. It will thus be seen that it is possible to draw up two specifications, each containing the same number of stops and the same number of pipes, but one may cost two or three times as much as the other, and its artistic value may be represented by a still larger ratio of difference.

Specification of small organ.

For small churches, seating from six hundred to eight hundred people, it would be far better to select a thoroughly good two-manual organ with from nine to twelve stops than to listen to the importunities of a builder who offers twice the number of stops for the same price. A good organ, even if limited in scope, will interest a musicianly organist and tend to retain him. The following specifications of a nine stop organ really contain the best parts of an instrument of much greater size:

Great Organ.

	FEET.
Open Diapason	8
Gamba	8
Doppel Flute	8

Swell Organ.

	FEET.
Violin Diapason	8
St. Diapason	8
Salicional	8

Flute 4
Oboe 8

Pedal Organ.

Bourdon. 16

This scheme, with pneumatic action, permitting the addition of sub and super octave couplers, would give great variety and ample power if properly constructed. Each fundamental quality of organ tone is well represented, the diapason tone by the Open Diapason and the Violin Diapason, the string tone by the Gamba and the Salicional, and the flute tone by the Dopped Flute, the Stopped Diapason, the 4-foot Flute and the pedal Bourdon, and the reed tone by the Oboe. The Oboe would be equally useful as a solo stop, in combination with other stops, or in the full organ, where it would add color and richness. Such an organ from the best makers would cost quite as much as the ordinary organ of twice the nominal stop capacity, but the latter would be vastly inferior in body and in quality, and would be overladen with cheap four and eight foot stops. A con- congregation takes both pride and pleasure in the possession of a really fine instrument, and it would be a constant incentive to devotion by leading in the hymns, by enriching the work of the choir, and by appealing to the finer emotions through well-selected voluntaries.

Durability of a first-class organ.

Incidentally many a repair bill would be saved and the choir would be spared the embarrassment of depending upon a faulty and uncertain instrument.

A poor instrument is a constant irritant to the musically sensitive and a never-ending source of dissatisfaction to all concerned. The more capable the organist, the more ready he will be to accept the first position which offers a better organ. The inadequacy of his instrument will be a constant damper to his ambitions both as a player and a choirmaster. The members of the choir will have the discouraging feeling that their best efforts are more or less discounted by the organ, and there is always the possibility of the mechanism getting out of gear at the most inopportune moments. The real value of such an instrument is discovered when an attempt is made to dispose of it.

A word as to the care of the organ. Most organ or music committees are disposed to think that after an organ has been purchased and installed, especially if it is from the hands of a prominent and reliable maker, that nothing remains to be done. If an organ were kept in a room of even temperature and reasonably free from dust and dampness it would require but little attention indeed. Unfortunately it is generally placed in a building where the temperature may vary in twenty-four hours from the

freezing point to seventy degrees. An organ is Sensitiveness.
far more sensitive to changes in temperature
than a piano, for it is far more complicated and
delicate. Dampness is its arch-enemy, dust and
smoke it cannot endure, and rats, mice, or cats
can do it endless mischief. It therefore stands
to reason that if the organ is not safeguarded
against these various evils trouble will result
even with the very best constructed instrument.
Take the matter of tuning, for example. It is
usually done on Saturdays before the church is Variation of temperature.
warmed up to the Sunday standard. The tuner
will leave it in good shape, but a change of ten
degrees will spoil all his work, for wood and
metal are affected differently by changes of temperature.   In fact, the organ is so sensitive that
it may be in tune at the beginning of a service
and be badly out before the close, if the temperature is raised considerably by the presence of
the congregation. The excessive changes in a
building which is only heated up once a week
are also trying to the mechanism, and it is no
cause for wonder if something goes astray.

Variations of temperature, however, are not Dampness.
so trying as dampness. We all know how that af-
fects our household furniture, and when we consider that several scores of keys are connected
with several hundreds of pipes, not to mention
the stop action, it is really a matter of surprise
that organs behave as well as they do, consider-

ing how ill they are treated. Organs are still placed in pockets or recesses where proper ventilation is impossible and where the normal temperature of the building never penetrates. As a result the metal rusts, the wood swells, the leather decays. Under these conditions a poor organ is apt to have one advantage over a good one for the reason that the woodwork is green and will not absorb as much moisture. The simple expedient of a burning lamp or two in an organ chamber (with proper ventilation), has been known to revolutionize the working capacity of a troublesome instrument.

Cleaning. An organ should also be periodically cleaned in order to keep it in favorable playing condition. This is usually left until it is an imperative necessity and then the much abused instrument will need extensive repairs to pay for the neglect. The thorough cleaning of an instrument is a matter that can only be undertaken by organ builders, for it necessitates the dismantling of the pipes, the opening of the wind chests, and a general dismembering of the action. A superficial dusting of the surface accumulations of dust is a very dangerous thing to do, for it is apt to remove it from places where it is doing no especial harm to the inner mechanism, where it will do a great deal of harm. For this reason an organ tuner moves about with great circumspection when pursuing his work. When one takes into account the wholesale neglect to which organs are generally subjected it is certainly a matter of surprise that so many instruments render fair service Sunday after Sunday.

Up to some forty years ago, organs in this country were supplied with tracker actions, a system which connected the keys with the pipes by means of narrow strips of wood. For small organs this system was quite satisfactory and is in use to the present day. In large instruments, however, the duplication of this mechanical device for several keyboards makes the action so heavy that it is well-nigh unplayable. This led to the invention of the pneumatic action already mentioned, and later to a combination of electric and pneumatic action. By means of these systems the action is made as light or lighter than that of a piano, regardless of the size of the instrument. It is only in quite recent years that the electric action has been brought to that state of perfection that it can be absolutely relied upon. With its use the keyboard may be any distance from the instrument, or the various departments of the organ may be distributed in various parts of the building. Echo organs may be placed in distant towers or concealed in hidden chambers. The adaptation of electricity has also greatly increased the means of control and greatly lightened the labor of the or-

Tracker actions.

Pneumatic and electric actions.

ganist in the management of the stops and of other mechanical appliances. In fact this feature of organ building has been developed to such an extent that organists are beginning to cry "Hold! enough!" for it has arrived at such a degree of complexity that the human brain cannot contain it all. In the olden days an organist with a fifty-stop organ would have three manual keyboards, a pedal keyboard, six couplers, one swell pedal, and six or eight combination pedals to look after in addition to his fifty stops. Nowadays in the same size organ he will have his fifty stops, eighteen or twenty pistons, twelve or more couplers, as many combination pedals, two swell pedals, and a crescendo pedal. While all these appliances facilitate the manipulation of the organ, they also increase the chances of making slips, and a nervous organist is in constant trepidation lest some oversight will result in an unexpected explosion of sound. America has certainly outstripped Europe in the development of these mechanical appliances, but they are severely criticised by foreign organists, notably by Edwin H. Lemare, who is probably the greatest organ virtuoso living, and who is phenomenally clever in feats of registration and in the reproduction of orchestral effects. Mr. Lemare claims that Yankee ingenuity has overshot the mark and that many of these would-be aids to ready registration are in reality hindrances. A uniform system of control would be a great boon to organists, for they would then be saved the mental wear and tear of constantly learning new systems. Not only has every enterprising organ builder his own particular fads and fancies in the disposition of the stops, pistons, and levers, but he is continually improving, or at least changing, his own system. The following advice and criticism from the highest living authority may well be heeded by every American builder: *[Uniform system of control desirable.]*

> "In America I have found many good organs. They are especially effective in the softer stops, such as the Dulciana, Flutes, and Gamba. But the full organ lacks resonance and does not thrill. I do not think the mixtures and reeds of the Great organ should be included in the swell-box, as this weakens the tone and destroys proper balance. The pedals in American organs are not so clear and distinct as they should be. They lack the 8-foot and the 4-foot tone. The effect is the same as if there were too many double basses in the orchestra and not enough 'cellos. The 16-foot Open Diapason in the Great organ is so powerful that every organ should have also the milder 16-foot Bourdon, which gives mellow quality to the foundation stops. But, as a rule, the softer 16-foot stops are wholly lacking in American organs. *[Guilmant's criticism.]*
>
> "Organ builders should devote less time to mechanical improvements, and more time to improving the tone of their instruments. Me-

chanical appliances are multiplying so fast that soon an organist will be unable to occupy himself with anything except the mechanism of his instrument. This is much to be deplored. Organ-playing should be essentially musical, and as far as possible in the pure style of the organ. It should not involve constant changes of registration. There is too much tendency to use vibrating stops—Vox Celeste and Vox Humana."

These words are from the pen of Alexandre Guilmant, and every truly musical organist will agree with him.

Solo playing more general in France. The organ as a solo instrument is used more extensively and systematically in the French Roman Catholic churches than in those of any other denomination or country. All the larger churches in Paris are provided with two organs: a small one in the chancel to accompany the choristers, and a large one over the main portal used chiefly for voluntaries. In the more prominent churches these gallery organs are famous and produce a thrilling effect with their full power despite the vastness of the edifices. On listening to organs such as these Honoré de Balzac, that masterful delineator of human character, has been moved to speak as follows:

Balzac's tribute. "The organ is in truth the grandest, the most daring, and the most magnificent instrument invented by human genius. It is a whole orchestra in itself. It can express anything in response to a skilled touch. Surely it is in some sort a pedestal on which the soul poises for a flight forth into space, essaying on her course to draw picture after picture in endless series, to paint human life, to cross the Infinite that separates heaven from earth. And the longer a dreamer listens to those giant harmonies the better he realizes that nothing save the hundred-voiced choir on earth can fill all the space between kneeling man and a God hidden by the blinding light of the sanctuary. The music is the one interpreter strong enough to bear up the prayers of humanity to heaven, prayer in its omnipresent moods, prayer tinged by the melancholy of many different natures, colored by meditative ecstasy, upspringing with the impulse of repentance, blending with the myriad fancies of every creed. Yes, in the long-vaulted aisles the melodies inspired by the sense of things Divine are blest with a grandeur unknown before, and decked with a new glory and might. Out of the dim daylight and the deep silence, broken by chanting of the choir in response to the thunder of the organ, a veil is woven for God, and the brightness of His attributes shines through it."

IV.

THE ORGANIST AND CHOIRMASTER.

Organists as a class are credited with being better musicians than pianists, singers, or players of orchestral instruments. The reason for this is not far to seek. The pianist, for example, rarely has further demands made upon his artistic, theoretical, or technical equipment than the effective performance of a fixed task. In the practical pursuit of his profession it is not ordinarily necessary that he read music well at sight or that he be able to transpose readily. To be sure, we read of astonishing feats at the piano, such as Liszt's wonderful power in seizing at a glance the essential features of a full orchestral score and transcribing it on the instant for the key-board, or of Brahms transposing the entire Kreutzer Sonata a half tone lower when confronted with an instrument tuned too high; but these men were composers as well as pianists. The professional accompanist should surely be able to meet any reasonable demand of the singer for a change of key, but to the average pianist transposition is an unknown art and the ability to read readily at sight exceptional. Then the pianist's knowledge of harmony, counterpoint, and composition is rarely called into practical use, and he may enjoy a world-wide reputation as a virtuoso and have very scant knowledge of the theoretical side of his art.

Not so with the professional organist. If he has a post of any importance at all and is capable of filling it in any adequate way, he must be well equipped. Not infrequently is he called upon to play difficult accompaniments without preparation. He is expected not only to play them correctly but to adapt himself to the idiosyncrasies of the singer and be ready to rally at any moment to his support should he show any signs of weakness or uncertainty. For singers are the least reliable of all musicians, and if they sing at sight it is apt to be after the fashion of the famous singer whose abilities in that direction were tested by the great Handel, and after an ignominious failure the candidate still protested that he could sing at sight—but not at first sight.

Organists must read well at sight.

Singers poor readers.

Then the capable organist should at least have the ability to play the choral service, the hymns and chants in any desired key. If the service is sluggish and dull a little higher **pitch**

Organists must transpose.

will put new life into it. If the choir or congregation is flatting in the chanting or hymn-singing, a rousing interlude and a change of key will invariably improve the situation. Many priests in intoning the service will have a strong tendency to change to a more convenient pitch, and it is the part of wisdom for the organist to accommodate him, rather than be continually trying to "boost" him to the proper key. The clergy sometimes get credit for phenomenal ability in striking the right pitch, when in point of fact it is the cleverness of the organist in adapting himself to the pitch of the priest that is phenomenal. As many of the older organs are tuned to the old Concert Pitch (which is nearly a semi-tone above the present International Pitch), many organists will transpose difficult *Te Deums* or anthems that they may be sung nearer the key intended by the composer, and that the choir may be relieved from the strain of the higher pitch.

Organists must harmonize at sight.

Then the good organist should be able to harmonize a tune well at sight, or to vary the harmonies to a hymn or chant when they are sung in unison. To do this in good taste and with a ready facility requires not only a thorough understanding of the complicated arts of harmony and counterpoint, but also an inborn intuitive taste. Hymn singing may be transformed by a good organ accompaniment, and if a congregation is taught to understand that an organ interlude is an indication that the succeeding verse is to be sung in unison, inspiring climaxes may be effected through the use of richer harmonies and freer modulations.

Again, the organist must be ready to improvise at a moment's notice in order to fill in any unexpected gaps in the service. To do this artistically calls upon an intimate acquaintance with the laws of composition and decided gifts of imagination and conception.

Lastly, the organist must have a feeling for tone color and a knowledge of orchestral effects. The organ is the only instrument controlled by one player which contains radically different qualities of tone. It is in fact a collection of many instruments which can be used singly or in combination. The piano has been likened to a photograph with its infinite gradations of light and shade, but all of one tone, while the orchestra suggests the richness and variety of color in an oil painting. Although the organ lacks the plasticity and finish of the orchestra, still its possibilities in the way of tonal variety are great and it is the only instrument that approximates in any way orchestral effects. While any single instrument of the orchestra will exceed in beauty of tone and expressiveness the corresponding tone quality in the organ, still the latter with all its restrictions often offers an effective substitute for a full orchestra, and it possesses other qualities in the way of sustained grandeur which adapts it to the peculiar needs of Church music far better than an orchestra.[1]

How is the organist educated to fit him for such an arduous and exacting task? For he must not only be a good musician theoretically, but also have skill as an executant of a high order. In England, that land which excels all others in fine organs and clever organists, in the beauty of its musical services and in the grandeur of its churches, it is managed in one of two ways. Either the would-be organist enters a good school of music where he receives a thorough training in the various branches belonging to the profession, or (as has been the experience of most of the celebrated English organists) he becomes an "articled pupil" of some Cathedral organist. An "articled pupil" is always some talented youth who is accepted as a musical ward by the skilled specialist who has charge of the organ and music of one of the numerous English Cathedrals. The lad receives his entire musical education at the hands

----

[1] The varied demands which are made upon the musical resources of the organist are apt to stimulate his musical fancy, and this no doubt accounts for the fact that the great majority of American composers come from the ranks of the organ players. MacDowell is perhaps the only prominent exception, but such composers as Dudley Buck, Horatio Parker, George W. Chadwick, Arthur Foote, and a host of lesser lights bear testimony to the accuracy of the statement.

of this specialist, and in return the instructor commands the services of his pupil, who sooner or later becomes assistant organist. The pupil is nearly always from the ranks of the choir, and he thus has, from his early youth, the unequalled advantage of hearing nothing but the best of Church music performed in an exceptional manner. He grows up in an atmosphere of good ecclesiastical art and is familiar with the best traditions. Given a moderate amount of talent and industry he cannot help but develop into an excellent organist and choirmaster. From the American point of view an organist thus trained is apt to be rather hidebound by his traditions and lacking in force and enterprise, but his thorough knowledge of the service, his smooth style of playing, and his regard for the dignity of the service are perhaps better assets than American energy and initiative, combined as it so frequently is with a lack of sound, musical Churchmanship.

The Cathedral system of England has been a veritable nursery for the development of Church music, and all who have had the privilege of learning the results of the system will readily admit its superiority. A large majority of the prominent English composers have come directly from the ranks of Cathedral choirs or from those of the Chapels Royal. Sir John Goss, George T. Smart and Edward J.

Hopkins were all products of the Chapel Royal at St. James' Palace, London; while Joseph Barnby came from York Cathedral and Sir John Stainer from St. Paul's, London. A lad of musical sensitiveness is fortunate indeed if he fall under the influence of such a system in his early youth, for it means the unconscious absorption of the best expression of religious music, and the acquirement of standards of judgment which will be invaluable in after life.

American opportunities. But what does the would-be organist of our great Middle West do if he wishes to thoroughly prepare himself as an organist and choirmaster? Music schools there are in plenty and excellent work is done in some directions, but none of them offer anything like an exhaustive course in organ playing and choir directing so far as it concerns our own Church. We have no long-established Cathedrals whose services are acknowledged types of the best usage, and the post of organist is of such uncertain tenure that the "articled pupil" system is all but impossible.

Development of American organist. The development of the average American organist is somewhat after this fashion: On exhibiting a little interest in music in his childhood he will have some desultory piano lessons, usually from a young woman of very limited attainments. When he gets into his teens the organ attracts him. With very inadequate technical preparation he will take organ lessons from a local organist. If he lives in a fair-sized city he may receive very good instruction as far as organ playing in concert is concerned, but the chances are that he will acquire next to no knowledge of Church music in general, and even less of the especial music of the Episcopal Church. His principal energies will be bent upon concert-playing, and if he is fairly capable and a good worker he will, by the time he has turned into the twenties, be able to give very respectable organ recitals. If he secures a position in a denominational church and is at all resourceful he will get along fairly well, but if he accepts a position in one of our own churches with any pretensions to a good choral service he will soon realize the inadequacies of his training. He will know nothing of the traditions of the choral service and will have difficulty with the simplicity of Tallis' responses. The chanting of the canticles and psalms will be more complicated to him than the playing of a Bach fugue, and Gregorians will be a veritable *bête noire*. He will have had no experience in improvising, modulating, transposing, or off-hand harmonizing. The order of the service, especially a choral celebration, will be an inextricable maze, and the conclusion will be forced upon him that he has been very poorly prepared for his profession as far as the

Difficulties of the Episcopal service.

Protestant Episcopal Church of America is concerned. He will also discover that this same Church is the only one with any definite musical system or standards, that music is an integral and important part of the service, and that special training and talent are required on the part of its organists and choirmasters. In consequence of these conditions he will furthermore learn that the Episcopal Church offers a far more interesting and lucrative field than the sectarian Churches.

The fundamental mistake in this organist's education has been that he pursued his work purely from the secular side and no attention had been paid to it as a ministry of the Church. Church organists should be primarily Churchmen and secondarily musicians, but sad to relate the reverse is the rule and there are all-too-many organists whose interest in religion has reached the vanishing point. The interest of this large class of organists is principally confined to the pleasure and satisfaction they get out of the purely musical side of their work. They may have, and frequently do have, excellent taste as regards Church music, but the proper attitude of mind is lacking. Even our sectarian brethren have been stirred by this prevailing irreligion among organists and choir directors, and the Congregationalists, at least, have attempted to improve the situation. They have founded an affiliated school of music with one of their Theological Seminaries, the avowed intention of which is to teach the theological students something about music and its relation to religion, and the musical students something about religion and its relation to music. It is a lamentable fact that organists who are first concerned about the fitting worship of Almighty God according to the best of their musical gifts are few indeed, while the opposite type, who use their positions to exploit their own cleverness, and who consider a church as primarily a place to give recitals in, are all too numerous.

When we reflect that the development of Churchly musical services after the English model has taken place only within the past half century, and when we take into consideration the fact that the American Church makes no provision whatever for the training of its musicians, it is not surprising that there should be such a dearth of good organists and choirmasters.

Dearth of good organists and choirmasters.

While we do not have the English Cathedral system in its completeness to develop our musicians, still our vested choirs serve as a base of supply and a preliminary training school for our future Church musicians. Many of the best and most successful organists and choirmasters in New York are "old Trinity boys,"

Vested choirs a training school.

while here in Chicago we have already direct results from the ranks of the pioneer vested choirs of this city among our prominent musicians. If this early start in the choir ranks could only be followed up by a comprehensive course in a well-equipped diocesan school of Church music our musical future would be more promising. An ideal school of such a type should be well-endowed and under the guidance and supervision of a musician of wide experience, superior training, and above all, sound Churchmanship. This institution would naturally be associated with the Cathedral of the diocese. The Cathedral, if possible, should maintain daily choral services of a high standard which should serve as practical models to the musical students. Not only should expert organists be trained in such an institution, but special attention should be given to the art of developing the boy voice, an art that is but little understood in this country.

The organist divides with the officiating priest the responsibility for the religious atmosphere of the church service. By well-considered voluntaries, by an earnest desire to swell the hymn of praise or deepen the fervor of prayer, he may materially augment the ministrations of the priest and sensibly aid the devotions of the congregation. On the contrary, by beginning divine worship with an irrelevant or trifling organ selection, by playing the chants or hymns in a careless or flippant manner, or by making evident a desire to "show off" the organ or his own performance, he can seriously disturb the reverent impulses of the people and nullify in a measure the efforts of the priest.[2]

It is a matter of astonishment how little attention is paid to the selection of voluntaries and how little considered is their fitness to the rest of the service. In England and Northern Germany, at least, better standards prevail, and the typical American custom of playing a sentimental Romance or Serenade on the Oboe with Tremolo for an opening voluntary, would hardly be tolerated. Nor would the noisy march for a closing voluntary meet with greater favor. The whole question is most pertinently summed up by the Rev. Howard Duffield, D.D., of the First Presbyterian Church, New York City, who is himself an organist and musician

Selection of voluntaries.

Dr. Duffield on the organ voluntary.

---

[2] Only recently the writer attended service in a prominent church in a large Eastern city. To his utter amazement and disgust the organist played a sensuous and impassioned love song from Saint Saens' "Samson and Delilah" while the congregation were receiving the Holy Communion. As if this were not a sufficient insult to every instinct of decency or reverence, it was followed by a selection that (unintentionally, let us hope) at once suggested the principle motive in Richard Strauss' "Til Eulenspiegel," a fantastic orchestral composition which humorously depicts the adventures of a freakish imp who is finally hung for his tricks. It was at least some relief to learn that the regular organist was ill and that these atrocities were perpetrated by an assistant. But it was none the less a most painful and trying experience.

of ability. In the "Church Economist" he speaks as follows:

"The usual method of closing the church services by a noisy outburst of organ music seems to have been specially planned to dissipate any spiritual impression which may have been produced. It is hard to conceive of a better scheme for promptly and effectively obliterating all the influences of the worship hour. The prayers have soothed and strengthened the heart; the holy song has banished the discords of life and winged the soul with new courage; the open Scriptures and the earnest sermon have searched and thrilled the soul, and brought wider vision, and larger hope, and braver purpose. The whole being, quickened with the brooding consciousness of coming very near to God in the sweet shelter of His House, bows for the benediction, and longs to carry away as in abiding possession the light and comfort of this holy hour. Bang-whang-whang goes the drum; tootle-te-tootle the fife.

"The amen from the pulpit is the signal for a blizzard of sound. The 'Postlude' must be played instantly and thunderously. Every stop is drawn, the manuals are coupled, the full organ blares and roars fortissimo, and every religious idea goes to the winds helter-skelter, like leaves in a cyclone. Custom has decreed that the service must be followed with musical din; that the hallowed silence of the peace unspeakable which has been stealing into the soul must be roared and clamored away; that every resolution and aspiration and feeling of fellowship with Christ shall be stunned, dazed, overwhelmed, swept out of existence by an untimely and meaningless Niagara of noise. Worshippers are habitually hustled out of God's House amid the roaring of a 'Fanfare,' or a 'Grand Choeur,' or 'Sortie,' or 'Fantasia,' or worse, but always something *fortissimo* and *allegro,* which means, being Englished, 'as loudly as you can and as quickly as you can drive away all holy thought and purpose.'

"This postlude habit amply justifies the Scottish antipathy to the 'kist of whistles.' To compel an organist to follow the benediction by an instant opening up of his organ to its utmost power of reverberation is neither rational, nor devotional, nor musical. It is not *rational* because it is a sheer waste of good music and trained skill. No one pretends to listen to a postlude. Should one desire to do so he can only catch a fragment while on his march to the door. The power of the organ is being exhibited and the ability of the organist is being taxed under circumstances which absolutely prevent their accomplishing any good result, or even of being appreciated at their true worth. It is not *devotional.* One of the most able and experienced of soul winners has termed the loud postlude 'a characteristic specimen of satanic ingenuity.' In its great moments the soul seeks quiet and shrinks from noise. When the depths of the heart are stirred the outburst of such a racket smites, like a blow on the face. It is not *musical.* The artistic sense revolts at it as utterly as the devotional sentiment. A master musician aptly described it as 'reducing music to the function of a door mat.' It is based upon the assumption that the organ has no higher possibility as an adjunct of divine worship than to drown the shuffling feet of the congregation as it assembles or disperses. A well-known director of church music recently remarked that if he played at all after church the people were sure to talk; if he played loudly they talked loudly, if he played softly they talked softly; but no one ever attached any meaning to the music, or seemed to suppose it accomplished any higher purpose than to give them a chance of talking without being heard.

"The organ can be so used as to intensify the spirit of worship. It can be employed as a potent aid in deepening devotion, and uplifting feeling, and carrying home into the depths of the soul the impressions which have been awakened by the service hour. After hymns have been sung, and Scripture read, and the sermon preached, and a word of prayer offered, there comes a natural pause in the moment of the service, when the sound of the voice, whether in speech or song, may well be hushed, and be succeeded and supplemented by the heart-warming and soul-searching ministries of music. The soul has been uplifted to God in song, has listened to God in His Word, has meditated upon God at the call of His servant, has spoken to God in prayer; and it instinctively demands that for a few moments, before it leaves the holy church's calm, it should be still and know God.

"Just here the organ can preach. Just here the introduction of carefully selected and well interpreted music will do more than speech could; will carry home to deeper depths every good impression; will touch, kindle, expand, uplift the soul and atmosphere the entire service with an influence in which it shall long continue to move." [3]

The matter of accompanying the Church service can, on the one hand, be discharged in a mechanical and perfunctory manner, while on the other it may call upon all the resources of a highly-skilled and sensitive musician.

Those parts of the service which are ordinarily considered of the least consequence are precisely the places which require the greatest thought and preparation. Take for example the chanting of the canticles and psalms. How often will an organist use the same registration from the beginning to the end of a psalm! Whether it expresses praise, aspiration, hope, trust, devotion, penitence, or contrition is all the same to his careless and thoughtless soul. If he have an organ of only moderate size he has a considerable variety of combinations at his command. Like a painter with his palette of colors he can mix his various qualities of tone and by their subtle use can intensify the varying shades of religious emotion. Given a large modern organ with its wealth of stops and

---

[3] Travelers relate that in the Philippine Islands "Tammany" and "A Hot Time in the Old Town To-night" are favorite voluntaries, and are played during the most solemn parts of the Mass in the Roman churches. The churches of Italy, especially the southern portion, have scarcely higher standards, for one frequently hears operatic overtures and dance tunes even in famous Cathedrals.

mechanical accessories, all the more scope will be given to the versatile and artistic organist to vary the usual deadly monotony of chanting.

On the other hand, abrupt, ill-considered or kaleidoscopic changes of registration are even greater violations of good taste than monotony, and the organist who attempts to musically picture the dramatic words of the psalms should not be tolerated. To illustrate in a realistic manner on the organ such passages as "One deep calleth upon another because of the noise of the water pipes," "Ye mountains that ye skipped like rams," "They go to and fro in the evening, grin like a dog and run about the city," or the description of the plagues of Egypt, are the height of absurdity and turn Divine worship into ridicule.

It is the emotional content of the psalms that the accompanist must seize and that in a broad-minded and comprehensive spirit. A too finicky and detailed interpretation will defeat its own purpose, for the force of contrast will be lost by over-elaboration.

Accompaniment of Gregorians. One of the most difficult tasks the organist has to cope with is the accompaniment of the Gregorian chants. To retain their innate characteristic they should always be sung in unison and this leaves the organist free to display his musicianship and taste in supplying varied harmonies. Nothing is more reprehensible than the custom of dressing up these ancient plainsong melodies with modern chromatic harmonies. The Gregorian modes represent a development of music totally foreign to our modern scales and chordal material. The average organist knows next to nothing of the ancient ecclesiastical modes, and is not at all familiar with the spirit in which they were conceived. In his ignorance he supplies them with nineteenth century harmonies, which is as much of an anachronism as to robe a Madonna with the latest Paris gown. Gregorians cannot be properly accompanied without a close familiarity with the rules of modal counterpoint, and their real force and character are lost without such accompaniment.

Then the effectiveness of hymn singing is at the mercy of the organist. An indifferent, careless style of playing, without definite rhythm or clear-cut phrasing, will not invite hearty coöperation on the part of the choir or congregation. Many organists consider the playing over of a tune a matter of no moment and in consequence it is done in either a slovenly and inaccurate manner or with mechanical and unmeaning precision. A hymn-tune should always be announced at the rate of speed in which it is intended it should be sung, and in accordance with the general emotional character of the text. To particularize: if a hymn be in

Accompaniment of hymns.

a jubilant vein, it should be given out with a fair amount of organ and with sufficient energy to put the congregation in the right spirit before it is taken up by them. On the contrary, hymns of a quiet and reflective nature should be played over on a more subdued organ and in a more deliberate manner. This, however, must not be construed in too sentimental a manner so that the tune loses its rhythmic outline and swing.[4]

The prevailing spirit of each stanza should be suggested by the organ, avoiding a too literal and minute exposition. Sudden transitions from loud to soft are in bad taste and tend to discourage timid singers. A hymn should be treated as a coherent and logical whole, and the ebb and flow of sentiment should be confined to reasonable limits. A well-planned climax is always effective and should be made use of whenever the text permits.

Good hymn playing rare.

Good hymn playing is rather a rare accomplishment and calls upon a sensitive nature that is keen to realize and anticipate the needs of the moment. As a rule, congregations musically are a sluggish and inert mass moving along the line of least resistance. The organist must infuse life and enthusiasm into this mass, and this requires a certain aggressiveness on the

---

[4] One of the most difficult tasks is to play music in moderate or slow tempo and to maintain the rhythmic unity of the larger pulses.

part of the player. He must take the reins into his own hands and as unobtrusively as possible guide the singers. He must exercise all the ingenuity at his command to arouse choir and congregation into a spirit of active coöperation, and by his well-directed domination see to it that the hymn singing does not degenerate into a perfunctory and meaningless office.

A few practical hints may be useful to inexperienced organists. One of the commonest faults is to keep the pedals forever booming, and when to this is added the atrocious habit of playing mostly in the lowest octave it becomes well-nigh intolerable. Give the pedals a rest once in a while on the quieter verses and observe what a fine effect they have when added dignity and weight are desired. Save the lowest tones for special climaxes or the final summing up. Use the Great organ in its varying degrees of power alone occasionally, for many keep it coupled to the swell practically all the time. If the alto or tenor is particularly melodious for a phrase or two, bring it out on a separate manual. The melody may be played as a solo either as written or an octave higher or an octave lower. In the latter case it is especially effective as a trumpet solo (plus diapasons) against the full swell. Contrast diapasons against reeds, strings against flutes, etc.

In the accompaniment of the anthem and

Practical hints on hymn playing.

Accompaniment of anthems.

the service numbers the organist can show his art to the highest advantage. As a soloist he rarely has opportunity to shine. The opening and closing voluntaries are but casually listened to, and set organ numbers during the service are becoming more and more the exception. In accompanying a good choir the organist is not hampered by the restrictions placed upon him in hymn-playing, where he is obliged to support the voices. He can freely use the entire resources of his instrument in lending color and variety to his work. The art demands as keen a sense of literary as of musical values, for the object is not alone to enhance the effect of the music by every legitimate means, but to enforce the meaning of the words as well.

The art of accompaniment of prime importance.

The art of good accompaniment and the ability to improvise are of far more practical value to the Church organist than great gifts as a concert player. The true spirit of devotional music is more in evidence while accompanying the monotoned parts of the service than in the most elaborate anthems or canticles. The Lord's Prayer, the Creed, the priest's part in the Litany are the delight of the real Church organist. It is his part not to make the organ conspicuous, or to call attention to his own cleverness, but to so reinforce the voice of supplication, of faith, or of praise that his own earnestness may be apparent to all susceptible hearts.

The organist is frequently called upon to fill in gaps in the service which would otherwise pass in awkward silence. Here again the artistic touch and the reverent nature should be in evidence. The playing of pretty but incongruous melodies, or the exploitation of the Vox Humana with sentimental but meaningless phrases, should be avoided. One of two principles should be adopted for the improvisation to be in thorough good taste. The music should either embody a reference to what has gone before, or suggest what is to come. In other words, the organist should have the ability to develop or enlarge upon the musical themes which immediately precede or succeed the situation in question. Here is opportunity for the highest phase of the art of organ-playing, the art that welds the whole service into a coherent, connected, and artistic whole.

The art of improvisation.

In the choral celebration of the Holy Eucharist the greatest demands are made upon the resources and abilities of the organist. To so manage his part that the true spirit of reverence and devotion is never lost, to see to it that no balks or faults or hesitations mar the sacredness of this highest act of worship, to be alert and ready to off-set or mitigate the acts of carelessness or inefficiency on the part of others, is no small task or responsibility. Above all, the spirit of solemnity and devout

The choral celebration.

worship must be maintained until the very end
of the service, and no blatant or irrelevant postlude permitted to jar upon the "peace that pass-
eth all understanding."

Joachim, that greatest of violinists and musicians, contended that rhythm was the very
soul of music. Now the organ, from the very
nature of its mechanical construction, is the most
difficult of all instruments to extract rhythm
from, and the organist's constant aim should be
to overcome this fundamental lack as far as it
is possible to do so. It is quite possible to play
with well-defined rhythm on the organ, but this
is only accomplished by what might be termed
an excess of accuracy and precision. This being the case, what shall we say of the so-called
organist who is so unconscious of the importance of rhythmical integrity that he is constantly coming to a standstill with his music in
order to manipulate the stops! One invariable
dictum may be laid down: if the management
of the stops cannot be effected without breaking
the rhythm, let the registration go. Smoothness
and continuity are the indispensable features
of good organ playing, and it is the player's
business to maintain these essentials at all costs.
To hang on to a chord indefinitely with one hand
while the other is groping for stops is the acme
of bad organ-playing. A clever organist with
quick wits and trained muscles will do most as-

tonishing feats in stop manipulation without interfering in the slightest with the rhythmic flow of the music.

As a rule, changes in registration should coincide with changes of sentiment, and should begin and end with a definite phrase or section of the music.   In the orchestra we do not begin a musical sentence with a flute and finish it with a violin, nor do we find one instrument augmenting another in a haphazard way. Logic is as essential in esthetics as in ethics.

Registration.

A word of caution must be given in regard to the use of the swell pedal. This single means of varying the tone quantity of certain stops or combinations of stops must be used sparingly, or its effectiveness will be badly discounted. If one is continually "see-sawing" on the swell pedal, producing erratic gusts of sound, its legitimate use as a means of climax and artistic gradation of tone is completely frustrated. The typical self-instructed organist delights in pumping the swell pedal with his right foot, under the delusion that he is playing "with expression," while the left foot is vainly attempting to accomplish the impossible task of playing the pedal part smoothly with one foot. As in the case of excessive registration, the greater effect is destroyed by the smaller, and a total lack of artistic balance results.

The swell pedal.

The custom of frequently making use of the

The full organ. full power of the instrument is also pernicious and robs the player of one of his most potent means of effect. It should be saved for rare instances where special climax is desired, and then its full value will be appreciated. Mere noise for its own sake should never be indulged in—a brass band would serve that object far better.

It is a curious fact that bad taste and inexperience on the part of the organist are frequently accompanied by exaggerated mannerisms while playing. The trained artist will perform his difficult task with the least possible **Exaggerated mannerisms.** expenditure of effort, and his movements will be made deftly and quietly, whereas the tyro will give the impression that organ playing is an acrobatic task requiring great strength and agility. These herculean efforts greatly impress the uninitiated at times, but they are entirely unnecessary and not only distress and disturb the more sensitive-minded, but hamper the player and interfere with his own measure of success.

Relation of priest and organist. The relation of the organist to the priest in charge is always a delicate one. Both belong to professions which tend to sensitiveness and nervous tension. The organist naturally knows more of music than the minister, still, according to the canons of the Church, the latter has control of both organ and organist, and if he so choose, can dictate what music is to be used and how it is to be performed. Sometimes he knows nothing of music and does not hesitate to admit it. Again he may possess a highly gifted musical nature and have sufficient practical knowledge of the subject to be perfectly justified in whatever criticism or suggestions he may offer. Clergy of this latter type, however, are about as rare as the organist who is thoroughly posted in the ecclesiastical aspects of his profession and in thorough sympathy with them. The organist is altogether more prone to be interested in concert-playing or in music generally, than in his particular task of adapting himself to the ends and conditions which surround him. With all these differing factors presenting themselves in varying degrees there is endless opportunity for friction and misunderstanding. Frankness and forbearance will be necessary on both sides. The organist will do well to remember that when all is said and done, he has been engaged to perform a specific work more or less to the liking of those who pay his salary. But the clergyman is not to forget that a man who is willing to make sacrifices for his ideals and convictions is a valuable member of the community, and that these ideals and convictions are not the personal conclusions of the man concerned, but those of the best minds in the musical world, and as such deserve respect and consideration.   The matter has been aptly summed up in an address by a prominent clergyman of New York on the occasion of his election to the post of chaplain of the American Guild of Organists:

"Never give up one jot or one tittle of your ideals. But you have got to understand that if you can't get a whole loaf you had better take a half; that if you cannot do all that you want to do you had better do as much as you can. I may have very high ideals, but I have to take my fellow men as I find them. I may have the highest ideals of music and I insist upon holding them, but it does not follow that a plain, simple little sermonette hasn't its value in the spiritual life of the people, and it is also perfectly evident that some simple, pathetic, beautiful little song, which may not be very good musically, has also its place and light in the life of the people. Hang on to your ideals. I would not give a snap of my finger for a man who had no great views of his life's work and thoughts of the music he wants to give, but he must remember that he is dealing with people, many of whom are utterly ignorant of music, many of whom dislike it, and only a few really appreciate it. And he has got to guide his life not only with reference to his ideals, but with reference also to the capacity of the people with whom he is dealing."

The choir-master.

Thus far the office of organist has alone been considered. It is usually combined with that of choirmaster, and the dual position calls for a combination of qualities that is rare indeed. An efficient choirmaster must also be a good musician and in addition be an expert voice-trainer, a skilled instructor, and above all, possess the qualities which attract and interest. Exemplary character and good Churchmanship are even more essential in the choirmaster than in the organist, for he should not only train those under him in Churchly singing, but he should also be responsible for their moral and religious development. Without reverence for the Church and love of the work for its own sake, satisfactory results will never be attained. In this regard we may well learn from the Lutherans, who make it a rule to permit neither organist, choirmaster, or singer to take part in their services who is not a member of their communion.

It is in the matter of voice-training where nine-tenths of our choirmasters are deficient, and where one person is both choirmaster and organist the situation is not at all improved, for the latter is usually three-fourths organist and one-fourth choirmaster. In other words, the individual concerned is nearly always attracted to the work through the fascinations of the organ. That instrument he studies with a certain degree of thoroughness, and when he finds it necessary to include choir-training in his activities, instead of properly preparing himself for that he trusts to his native wit and general musicianship. The

Knowledge of voice culture essential.

Organists poor voice trainers.

matter of discipline cuts such a figure in the situation, that given a fair organist and the ability to organize and control a choir, the question of proficiency as a voice trainer is not much in the foreground. To take a boy off the street and to change his natural inclination to yell in his chest tones to habits of really good and correct tone production is a task so difficult that it borders almost on the miraculous. In addition to the necessary technical knowledge it requires infinite patience, tact, and unfailing good humour. It is the lack of this knowledge of how to produce good and agreeable tones that lies at the root of the general unsatisfactoriness of our so-called "boy choirs." As a rule, our boys do not sing—they shout or yell. One unconsciously gets into the mental habit of excluding the efforts of a boy choir from the category of real music. They are judged from standards other than those applied ordinarily to chorus singing. We have a subconscious feeling that doctrinal, utilitarian, or sentimental reasons exist which justify the use of the boy choir, no matter how much they may offend our ears or violate our artistic senses. And still some of the most esthetically exacting among us have heard choirs of men and boys which have more than satisfied our highest ideals, and have driven hard home the conviction that the vested male choir fills every requirement of an ideal service, both artistically and liturgically.

If this astounding gulf between our worst and our best choirs is largely a matter of ability to train the human voice, why is so little emphasis placed upon skill in vocal culture? The question can be answered in part by the fact that boy choirs are to a certain extent a fad. Every church, down to the smallest and poorest, must enjoy the picturesque spectacle of a surpliced choir, whether or not the conditions warrant it. Without a considerable appropriation for its maintenance, and without an environment that will supply good material it is hopeless to expect results that will justifiy the effort, judged from any sane or unbiased point of view. **Boy choir a fad.**

But unfortunately there is generally some one who will undertake the running of a boy choir, even under the most adverse and unpromising conditions. If the organist declines, it is apt to be delegated to some enterprising person whose entire preparation for the exacting task consists in the fact that he at one time, as boy or man, sang in a vested choir. And the choir he sang in was probably an inferior one. In this manner inefficiency is added to inefficiency and deplorable traditions are established and perpetuated. As already hinted at, the ability to maintain a semblance of order among unruly **Incompetent volunteers.**

boys is of such practical value that many musical short-comings are almost gladly overlooked if discipline is maintained. But not infrequently we meet the combination of bad conduct and wretched singing, and surely in such cases the limit of Christian forbearance is reached.

The disciplinarian. The primary need of good discipline has evolved the choirmaster who has good executive ability and the knack of attracting, holding, and controlling choristers. With such a man in command everything moves with military precision, including the music. The choir entertainments and encampments are always a great success. The singers are well-drilled, but in a mechanical way. From some points of view such a man is a prize indeed and a great boon to the parish priest, for he relieves the latter of much responsibility and care. Choirmasters of this type, however, are usually lacking in the artistic sense. They have little judgment in the selection of suitable music and little feeling for its proper performance. Such refinements as good tone production, accurate intonation, and sympathetic interpretation do not enter within their horizon.

Professional voice teachers not available. One would think that a professional voice teacher would be the logical choice for a choirmaster, but such is not the case. There are several reasons for this. In the first place, it is difficult to make a boy comprehend the nice and complicated processes of voice production. The work is necessarily elementary and consequently uninteresting to most teachers. The responsibility entailed in taking charge of a lot of boisterous youngsters is not usually attractive. The training and developing of the boy voice is a special art in itself which the great majority of voice teachers know nothing about. Lastly, a really proficient vocal instructor can command such a sum for his services in instructing adults that even a good church salary fails to tempt him.

When the offices of choirmaster and organist are separated the choirmaster has charge. The organist is almost certain to be the better musician of the two and is placed in the trying situation of taking orders from a man less experienced musically than himself. It is only occasionally that the combination works out advantageously. The more capable the organist, the more anxious he will be to secure a position where he is his own master. The choirmaster is thus frequently forced to put up either with incompetent players, or frequent changes on the organ bench.

Organist subject to choirmaster.

The situation then, as regards our choirmasters has its complexities. Like our organists, they sadly need the aid of the Church itself. Our peculiar needs in Church music

Special training for choirmasters necessary.

are not to be found in any other Christian body, and the necessary experience cannot be gained outside our own walls. Surely the matter is of sufficient importance to demand the serious attention of the Church at large. One would naturally look to the clergy to take the initiative in such a cause. But it has been left to the laymen. At the last Conference of the Church Clubs of the United States held at St. Louis a paper was read severely criticising much of the music heard in our churches and suggesting that the matter be acted upon by the Conference. The result was the passing of a resolution to the effect that each Church Club of the country be asked to appoint a committee to consider the general subject of the music in our churches, and that each committee submit recommendations to a central committee. It is sincerely to be hoped that something practical and improving may be evolved from this scheme.

Any thorough sifting of the subject will make apparent the fundamental need of proper training schools for our organists and choirmasters, and the necessity of setting and maintaining proper standards of selection and performance. But any plan will fail of its purpose if it does not include the musical education of the clergy, so that they may intelligently guide and direct the musical forces over which they have control, and also have sympathetic appreciation for the artistic efforts of their co-laborers. It is both trying and discouraging for a musician trained in the best traditions of the Church and possessing high and praiseworthy ideals to be thrown into an environment where all his knowledge and experience go for little or naught. If he demurs at using music which he knows to be unseemly or unworthy, it is all the more to his credit. An exhaustive course in the appreciation of Church music should find place in the curriculum of every one of our theological schools, and the course should be obligatory. Even if the embryo priest should have no taste or love for music, he should at least be trained to understand that the choice of music for divine worship is too serious a matter to be left to the judgment of an uncultivated taste.

The question thus resolves itself into a campaign of education. The Church as a whole must be educated to that point where she realizes that she, in turn, must educate her priests, her organists, her choristers, and through them her people. In this way only can music receive its full meed of appreciation and rise to its full value as an aid to religion.

A closing word of a practical nature. A recent report of the corporation of Trinity parish, New York City, discloses the fact that over one hundred thousand dollars was expended in salaries for its clergy, and about sixty thousand dollars for its musicians during the preceding fiscal year. This, of course, included Trinity Church and the various chapels and missions. The statement makes plain the importance which the oldest, the largest, and the most experienced parish in the American Church attaches to its musical services, and it establishes a valuable basis for comparison. The appropriation of approximately one-half of the clerical salary list for music will be found to hold good in all churches where the music is at all satisfactory. This is of course based on the assumption that the clergy are adequately paid. The moment this proportion is materially reduced a church cannot in reason expect to secure the aid of competent musical talent. The best results are obtainable only where the musician in charge is sufficiently well paid to enable him to live comfortably without seeking other sources of revenue. If he is obliged to occupy himself otherwise during the week to any considerable extent, it will divide his interests and consume the energy and ambition that should be devoted to his church duties. If the resources of a church are insufficient to pay a living salary it is questionable indeed if that parish had better indulge in the luxury of a boy choir. There are other resources in every parish which will give far better results musically, and at much less expense both in time, trouble, and money.   But this aspect of the case will be considered in another lecture.

V.

The Vested Male Choir.

An English essayist remarks that if the old Athenian commander Timotheus should arise from the dead "he would be delighted with our post offices, interested in our railroads, ashamed of our oratory, horrified at our public buildings, but dumbfounded at our musical festivals."

His astonishment at the English musical festivals would probably suffer no abatement upon the discovery that in many instances the voices of young lads were responsible for the beauty of the general effect.   If he were interested in this aspect of the case he would further find out that the greatest Cathedrals in Europe entrusted the soprano part in their choirs not to the mature and emotional charm of women's voices, but to the pure tones and musical ability of lads ranging in age from ten to fifteen years.

It is a fact that the most famous choirs in existence, choirs that scorn the assistance of organ or orchestra, choirs noted for their beauty of tone and for the perfect manner in which they perform the most difficult scores of the great masters, invariably make use of the boy voice for the soprano and sometimes the alto part.

Whether we go to the Imperial Chapel at St. Petersburg, the Kremlin at Moscow, the Dom at Berlin, the Cathedral at Cologne, the Madeleine at Paris, St. Paul's or Westminster at London, King's College at Cambridge, or Magdalen at Oxford, we will hear lads sustaining their difficult parts with unerring accuracy, delighting the ear with the purity of their voices and satisfying the most exacting taste in their artistic interpretations.

The Church of St. Thomas at Leipzig, proud in the fact that the mighty Johann Sebastian Bach had charge of its music something less than two centuries ago, supports a choir of men and boys that sings the works of the great Cantor every Sunday in the year. And they are works of such complexity that well-equipped and experienced choral societies plume themselves upon the occasional performance of a Bach motette or cantata, not to mention the rare performances of his Passion according to St. Matthew or St. John, or his gigantic Mass in B minor.

All this testimony goes to prove the wonderful capacity and efficiency of boys, provided they are properly and sufficiently trained.

Therein lies the whole secret—properly and sufficiently trained. The boys who sing in these world-famous choirs ordinarily receive their entire education at the hands of the Church they serve. They are, of course, selected for their natural musical gifts, but boys of like capacity exist in all large cities and in considerable numbers. It is the daily musical training and the skilled attention they receive which is responsible for the wonderful results, and not the phenomenal qualities of the boys themselves.

Sight-reading ability. The sight-reading abilities of these boys put to shame many an adult professional. They read music as they read words. Hymn music is as child's play to them, and anthems and mottettes of no mean difficulty are sung through the first time without hesitation or fault. But it is the result of severe daily drill and of a life having music as its consuming activity.

English choir schools. The Cathedrals of England are supplied with Choir Schools where the young lads not only receive sound musical training but also a general education, superior to that given in the public schools. They are nearly all boarding schools and in return for a liberal education the pupils sing at the daily Cathedral services. Without such a perfect system of training schools the results obtained would be impossible. When we recall that England has some thirty Cathedrals distributed over her restricted area

and that music has been systematically cultivated in them ever since the Reformation—a period of over 350 years—it is small wonder that
she has such high standards of Church music
and that her Church people generally appreciate
these standards. Good boy voices were in such
demand in the middle of the sixteenth century
that a musical "press-gang" scoured the country
for boys with good "brestes" or voices, and they
were empowered to seize such boys for service
in St. Paul's Cathedral or the Royal Chapels.

These Cathedral services serve as models **Cathedral services as models.**
which are emulated by the parish churches, the
more important of which maintain services
quite up to Cathedral standards. Even if the
parish churches are not provided with choir
schools of their own they will experience no
difficulty in securing choir boys already trained,
for there are schools established for this special
purpose.

Contrast this enviable state of affairs with **Disadvantages of conditions in America.**
conditions as they exist in this country. We
have no historic background musically speaking,
no well-defined standards of performance, and
few acknowledged models. Thoroughly capable organists and choirmasters are rare. The
time given to the work is inadequate. Choir
boys already trained are almost an unknown
quantity, and choir schools are in their infancy.
The average choral service is performed in a

coarse, unmusical, and inartistic manner. No one takes any pleasure in it. It is considered the normal state of affairs, and if a vested choir is wanted, crudities must be put up with as a matter of course.

Average choir poor. With these conditions prevailing in the large majority of cases, it is not surprising that Church people of refined musical sensibilities are frequently repelled by our services, and it is difficult for them to believe that there can possibly be any real merit in the so-called "boy choir."

Best choirs not up to European Standards. It is true that in New York City one hears services of decided merit and in our larger cities there are choirs whose attainments are most commendable. Still the best of these do not compare with the famous choirs of Europe, and the question arises, Why cannot we, with our energy, ambition and natural resources, have choirs equal to the greatest?

Necessity of choir schools. The only possible way is by the establishment of choir schools, and this conclusion is gradually forcing itself upon the consciousness of our leading churches. Before giving the actual results of this conclusion, a short sketch of the introduction of the vested male choir into the Protestant Episcopal Church of America, and its development in our own diocese, may be of interest.

The first vested male choir that historians

have been able to trace seems to have been in St. Michael's Church, Charleston, S. C., in the year 1798. It is quite plausible that a Southern church should have been the first to transplant the English custom to these shores, for the Church was far stronger and lived more nearly up to the standards of the Mother Church in the Virginias and Carolinas than was the case in New England, where under Puritan domination the Church was poor and weak, or in New York, where the Dutch and French Reformed churches were in the ascendancy. Of the history or longevity of this first surpliced choir we know nothing. The second choir is not heard of until 1841 and then at Flushing, L. I. The Church of the Advent, Boston, is reported to have had a vested choir in 1859. As early as 1761 boys were made use of in "Old Trinity," New York, but they were not vested nor did they sit in the chancel, but in the gallery. In 1709, a parish Charity School was organized and for many years the children of the school, both boys and girls, led with their crude singing the metrical psalms, and sang an occasional simple anthem.

With the advent of Dr. Edward Hodges, the eminent English organist and composer, in 1839, a capable choir was for the first time organized. At first it consisted of boys, women, and men, who occupied places in the organ gal-

Historical Sketch. St. Michael's, Charleston, S. C.

Flushing, L. I.
Church of the Advent, Boston.
"Old Trinity," New York City.

Edward Hodges.

lery over the main portal. The women were gradually eliminated and early in 1859 had entirely disappeared. Dr. Messiter in his interesting "History of the Choir and Music of Trinity Church" gives an entertaining account of the well-nigh surreptitious methods by which the choir was gradually transferred from the gallery to the chancel, a process which was vigorously opposed by many of the congregation. Several sorties were made during week-day services before the singers were permanently intrenched behind the choir pews—but with the men to the front. The choir was still unvested and the question of surplices was also a matter of bitter controversy. It was happily solved by the appearance of the Prince of Wales upon the scene of strife, and in order not to offend his majesty, the choir was properly vested on the occasion of his attending service at Trinity on October 14, 1860. To prevent any possible embarrassment the vestments were worn the previous Sunday by way of dress rehearsal. On this occasion two loud reports were heard during the reading of the Second Lesson, and a musket ball fell in one of the pews, without hurting any one. Whether it was a hostile demonstration or not was never ascertained.

After Trinity's lead the use of the vested choir slowly extended to other parishes, but it was a quarter of a century before the professional quartette, that "baneful medium for the glorification of four people" as it has been aptly put, had all but disappeared.

In the west the honor of first introducing the vested choir and the choral service belongs to Racine, Wis. A Mr. Machin was appointed choirmaster at Racine College about the year 1862, and the simple service he introduced was the sensation of the hour by reason of its novelty. As none of the college clergy could intone, Mr. Machin did so himself, and he was consequently much looked up to for his superior abilities. Helmore's Psalter was used, but little else except hymns was attempted. He was succeeded by a Mr. Rowe, also an Englishman, and later by the head-master, Gerald R. MacDowell, who was very gifted as a choirmaster.

Development in the West.

Racine College.

Mr. Machin.

Mr. Rowe. Gerald R. MacDowell.

The material for the choir was drawn from the various schools, but the constant changes in the grammar school boys and the undeveloped voices of the college students left much to be desired in the general effect. The institution fell upon evil days financially, and the college department was finally abandoned. As the services were confined practically to the faculty and students this attempt at a proper musical service had but little influence on the Church at large.

A more potent and far-reaching endeavor to establish a permanent choral service was made in the year 1865, when Bishop Whitehouse, the second Bishop of Illinois, took possession of the then Church of the Atonement, and made it the Cathedral Church of the diocese, the first Cathedral foundation to be established in the United States.

Several attempts were made at this period to make use of boys' voices in other churches of Chicago, but vestments were not used nor was the choral service attempted. A man by the appropriate name of Mozart endeavoured to train boys to assist in the music of St. James' Church, the oldest parish in the city, but was unsuccessful. A better venture was made at Trinity Church, which was then on Jackson street where the Illinois theater now stands. Mr. W. D. Rowlands, who sang there as a boy, wrote in 1886 as follows concerning music at Trinity:

"I sang in Trinity Church choir twenty-one years ago (*i.e.,* in 1865). It was composed of boys exclusively. We numbered fifteen and were seated in the organ gallery over the entrance, seven on each side of the organ. I, being the soloist, had a seat beside the lady soloist in front of the organ, and used to feel especially favored. During the service when it came our turn to sing the curtains were always drawn so that we might be heard and not seen. We chanted the psalms, I singing the first verse and the choir responding, changing alternately. The chorister sat down stairs and we were left to our fate upstairs. We always managed to sing in tune and to keep good time. Members of the congregation often spoke of the thrilling impression it made on them—could only think of angels' voices sounding from heaven, vibrating through the rafters. The lady soloist always sang one selection at each service during the collection. I sang in the choir two years—it had just been started previous to my joining. I believe it was continued until the church was destroyed by fire (the great fire in 1871). Mr. Ludden was the name of the chorister. Prof. Cutler, I think, was the organist."

To return to the Cathedral. Mr. William Fitzhugh Whitehouse, a son of the Bishop, was an amateur organist and much interested in the choral service. A mixed choir already existed and occupied seats in the east transept under the leadership of a Mr. Tobey. Mr. Whitehouse collected some boys together and instructed them in the mysteries of chanting. They occupied seats in the west transept by the organ, a small and inefficient instrument, incapable of supporting the voices. Mr. Tobey had no sympathy with the boys and friction existed between the two choirs. The most agreeable part of the service musically was doubtless the fine voice of the Bishop's chaplain, the Rev. John Wilkinson. This unsatisfactory condition of affairs lasted for two years, when the mixed choir of men and women was dispensed with. Up to this time a small sum had been paid the singers, but the choir was now put upon a volunteer basis. In his address to the Diocesan Convention in 1867 the Bishop speaks of the choir as follows:

> "The music has risen to a chaste standard, and the well-trained choir of boys meets our expectations. These choristers will be put into surplices as soon as stall-seats can be prepared and a larger robing-room built."

In the fall of this year the Rev. John Harris Knowles of St. John's, Naperville, was appointed Canon Chaplain of the Cathedral. Canon C. P. Dorset was precentor of the choir and Mr. Whitehouse, organist. The surplices came before the larger robing-room, and in February, 1868, six boys, duly vested in long surplices, entered the chancel from the diminutive vestry room singing "Jerusalem, the golden," to Ewing's well-known tune. Shortly after Canon Knowles was induced to take charge of the choir, but much against his wishes. When a student in the General Theological Seminary in New York a few years before (1862), he had sung in Trinity Church choir under Dr. Cutler where he became familiar with many traditional usages in the English choral service and acquainted with the better class of Church music generally. His sensitive, artistic nature was greatly impressed by both the music and the dignified ceremonial that obtained at "Old Trinity." A man of unusual musical appreciation and judgment, he labored under the disadvantage of having had but meager training on the practical side of the art.

The establishment of a vested choir and a choral service required no little courage. It was an unheard of thing at that time and was looked upon as rank popery. It caused dissension and bitter feeling, and many left the Cathedral for other parishes. No capable or experienced choirmaster was obtainable short of importation from England, and no funds were at hand to pay a choirmaster in any event. So the energetic Canon set to work, gathered together what material was at hand, and what he lacked in professional training he atoned for in unbounded enthusiasm and fixity of purpose. Already at St. John's, Naperville, he had established a choral service and choral celebration in 1865, but with an unvested choir of men and women. When he came to the Cathedral the service was only partly choral, but soon the evening service was completely so, Tallis' Responses and Trinity Psalter being used.

The choir at first were seated in wooden kitchen chairs arranged choir-wise in the chancel, and wore long surplices without cassocks. Among the half-dozen men were two or three Englishmen—one of them an adult alto—who had sung in choirs in their native land. It seems incredible that a Bishop, two canons, and sixteen choristers all robed in the little vestry-

Opposition to vested choirs.

Pioneer work of Canon Knowles.

St. John's, Naperville, Ill.

First Cathedral choral service.

Unpretentious beginnings.

room off of the chancel, which is now the organ chamber, yet such was the case.

First solo boy.

The writer entered the choir in 1868, and was the first boy in the choir to sing the alto part as he was also the first boy to sing oratorio solos, an accomplishment that has since become of common occurence. A new three-manual organ soon followed the old one in the west transept and it was considered a grand instrument at the time of its installation. Its distance from the choir was somewhat of a disadvantage, a condition that was rectified some twelve years later by its removal to the present location.

Resourcefulness of Canon Knowles.

The resourcefulness of Canon Knowles was early manifested. For an anthem he would take a short psalm—the Twenty-third for example—and after selecting a melodious chant would have certain verses sung as solo, duet or quartette to contrast with the full chorus. It

First anthems.

was not long, however, before real anthems were attempted and such old-time English favorites as "Behold, how good and joyful a thing it is," by Kent, "I will lift up mine eyes unto the hills," by Whitfield, "By the waters of Babylon," Allen, were imported from London, as they were unattainable in this country at that time. Cutler's "Trinity Anthems" were also sung, and it is a pity that such a fine collection of sterling Church music has since fallen into disuse. Occasional trips to England added stimulus to the zeal and musical ambition of the Canon, and in the course of a few years complete musical Services were given, such as Smart in F, Armes in A, and Stainer in E flat.

The choir was strictly a volunteer organization and its function and importance were duly magnified. In 1870 the Cathedral Choristers' Association was formed with its quota of officials. As its printed constitution read, it was formed "to secure for the choral worship of Almighty God that attention which such a holy work demands; to insure the proper rendering of the same by careful preparation in rehearsals, and prompt and regular attendance at public services, and by organization to perpetuate and place on a firmer basis the volunteer choir of the Cathedral of SS. Peter and Paul."

Monthly business meetings were held and the junior choristers elected representatives, who attended these meetings with full voting powers. Choir picnics, excursions, and banquets were held, and choral services were given in other churches and communities, thus spreading a love and desire for the choral service. Prizes and medals were awarded at the annual Christmas festival of the Sunday school to worthy boys for attendance, progress in music, and reverential demeanor, and all received valuable gifts. Admission of juniors to the choir was effected through the use of a formal service laying stress on the sacredness of the office. At the Sunday School festival on Trinity Sunday selected choir boys would read from the lectern lessons illustrative of the Christian year. The choir increased in size until it numbered from thirty to thirty-five members.

First festival service.

The state of efficiency attained by the choir at this period is best shown by its first festival service, which was held in the Cathedral on November 30, 1870.[1]

> PROCESSIONAL, "Songs of Praise," arranged from a March by ....*Costa.*
> CANTATE AND DEUS MISEREATUR in A..... ....*Bridgewater.*
> ANTHEM, "Like as a Father"..........*Hatton.*
> GLORIA IN EXCELSIS from Twelfth Mass. .*Mozart.*
> SOLO, "O Thou That Tellest Good Tidings to Zion."
> SOLO, "But Thou Didst Not Leave His Soul in Hell.
> CHORUS, "Hallelujah"
> From the "Messiah," *Handel.*

Funeral of Bishop Whitehouse.

The funeral of Bishop Whitehouse was a memorable occasion, the music being of a most impressive and appropriate character. Canon Knowles had remarkable tact and taste in planning and executing ceremonials, and he was

---

[1] Simple daily choral services were held at this time coinciding with the opening and closing of the Cathedral Day School, the writer beginning his career as organist on these occasions with the limited repertoire of one hymn and one chant. He later became assistant organist to Mr. William Fitzhugh Whitehouse, and upon the resignation of the latter (at the time his father, the Bishop, died), he became organist.

equally successful in arranging the services at the consecration of Bishop McLaren on December 8, 1875. Seven or eight Bishops were present and a host of clergy. The choir acquitted themselves finely with Gounod's St. Cecilia Mass—then a novelty.

A number of standard anthems and services by such composers as Stainer, Barnby, Smart, Sullivan, Gounod, etc., received their first performance west of New York at the hands of the Cathedral choir under the guidance of Canon Knowles. That the attainments of the choir constantly increased is evidenced by a lecture on Church music given by the Canon on February 16, 1879. The church was packed and the lecture was repeated on March 11, following. The musical illustrations sung by the choir were as follows:

> GREGORIAN MUSIC: The Seventh and Eighth
>   Tones and the Hymn "Pange Lingua."
> ANGLICAN CHANTS: .... *Croft* and *Barnby.*
> HYMN MUSIC: .... *Cruger* and *Dykes.*
> ANTHEMS:
>   "O Where Shall Wisdom be Found,"..*Boyce.*
>   "Hosanna in the Highest,"........ *Stainer.*
> MUSIC FOR THE HOLY EUCHARIST: Gounod's St.
>   Cecilia Mass. Selections from *Barnby* and
>   *Garrett.*

It must be borne in mind that all this musical activity on the part of Canon Knowles was in addition to his regular priestly duties, and

Consecration of Bishop McLaren.

Illustrated Lecture on Church Music.

Devotion of Canon Knowles.

it was only at times that he had any assistance in this latter respect. It required great devotion and purpose, unflagging zeal and a world of patience. It was musical pioneering in every sense of the word, and Church music throughout the West received a great impetus through the courage, conviction, and high standards of this enthusiastic champion of good Church art. No trouble or expense was too great when musical ideals were concerned. A large, well-selected, and comprehensive musical library was largely paid for out of the Canon's slender purse, and if works were too expensive to buy or unobtainable, his own hand spent many weary hours in making MS. copies. His discriminating taste permitted nothing unworthy, and his whole-hearted consecration to the cause had its reward in setting a proper standard of Church music in its proper setting of a Cathedral.

Musical library.

The chorister of the old Cathedral days has many pleasant recollections stored in his memory: of picnics and excursions, of concerts and social gatherings. Two pleasant trips were made to Aurora, Ill., one at the laying of the cornerstone of a new church and a second to give a benefit concert. Several most enjoyable trips were made to Racine College on invitation of the lamented Dr. de Koven, where the singing of the Cathedral Choir was much admired. The Knights Templars' service at Grace

Social features.

Church and a special service for St. George's Society at the Cathedral were always picturesque and interesting occasions.

As in the case of "Old Trinity," New York, the Cathedral Choir has developed musicians of prominence who in all probability would have followed other pursuits had it not been for the early musical surroundings which brought forth talent and perhaps unsuspected ability. Nor was the bold stand in regard to a full choral service at the Cathedral without its effect throughout the diocese. Parishes with High Church proclivities were naturally the first to follow. On Christmas day, 1870, a vested choir of seventeen boys and eight men made their first appearance in the Church of the Ascension. This was shortly after Canon Dorset, the first precentor of the Cathedral, had been appointed priest there. The organist was Henry Pilcher, a former Cathedral boy. From the nature of the services at the Ascension, special stress was laid on the Mass music, and in later years under Father Ritchie with Harrison M. Wild as organist and choirmaster, the church became notable for its fine selection of Masses. Not only were the usual run of English Communion services used, such as Stainer, Monk, Dykes, but also adaptations from the Latin Masses of Weber, Mozart, Gounod, etc. The Ascension has the distinction of being the only

Development of musical talent.

Spread of vested choirs.

Ascension, Chicago.

Henry Pilcher.

Father Ritchie.

Harrison M. Wild.

Latin Masses.

Gregorians. church in the diocese to use a real Gregorian psalter (Redhead's) and to make persistent use of plainsong hymn tunes.

Calvary, Chicago. If the writer's memory is not at fault, Calvary Church followed next with the vested choir. The more prominent and aristocratic churches were slower in giving up their quartette choirs. **St. James', Chicago.** St. James' had elected Dr. Vibbert from the East as its rector, and he stipulated a vested choir as one of the conditions of acceptance. On May 4, 1884, after nine months of arduous drill under the direction of Mr. **John L. Hughes.** John L. Hughes, Chicago's first English choirmaster, the choir appeared in the chancel, and in regard to tonal quality and finish it surpassed all others in the diocese. Mr. C. E. **C. E. Reynolds.** Reynolds was the organist. Mr. Hughes soon resigned on account of ill health and the choir attained great proficiency and a most enviable reputation under the enthusiastic and devoted **William Smedley.** guidance of Mr. William Smedley. Grace **Grace Church, Chicago.** Church soon followed with a semi-choral evening service in October, 1884, the quartette choir singing in the morning and continuing until January 1, 1886, when the vested choir performed full duty. Then came the new St. **St. Clement's, Chicago.** Clement's Church, where, on November 23, 1884, at its dedication a vested choir of eleven boys and ten men sang a full choral service. **Canon Knowles.** Canon Knowles, who had severed his connection with the Cathedral, was priest, and the writer was choirmaster and organist.

The remaining churches in Chicago installed vested choirs in rapid succession and the custom spread to the smaller towns; even village churches are not content without some semblance of a "boy choir." It is an open question whether the movement is the result of a desire to conform to Churchly traditions, or whether the motive springs from a wish to emulate the larger parishes. If a surpliced choir always satisfied the ear as well as it does the eye, the veil of charity might well be drawn over the underlying impulse.

If a chancel choir must obtain there is no question but that it should consist of males. In this regard the Church patterns after the Temple service, where the choir consisted of males drawn from the tribe of Levi. Women and girls sang only in the congregation or in the court set apart for the use of women, but not in the sanctuary, to which our chancel corresponds. It is against all tradition, precedent, or practice in all the historic churches to permit women to perform priestly functions, and the services of a chancel choir can only be looked upon as an adjunct to the priestly ministrations at the altar. While the Church of Rome has allowed its music to become secularized to a certain extent, and has made extensive use of women singers, they have always been relegated to the gallery and naught but men and boys permitted in the chancel.

Practical reasons for male choirs. There are purely practical reasons for the use of male choirs. Boys and men are sturdier than girls or women and may be depended upon in all weather and at all times. It is no infrequent spectacle on a stormy night to find more people in the choir stalls than in the pews, and the worship of Almighty God proceeds undisturbed, as it should, regardless of weather or the presence of a congregation.

Other factors. Thus we have excellent reasons for the use of male choirs on account of their fitness, utility, and reliability. But other factors enter into the discussion. As has been before intimated, there is also a fundamental principle that in its public services the Church should only offer its best: its best in thought, diction, ceremonial, and material surroundings. This principle should certainly be extended both to music and the manner of its performance. With sufficient means and material this end is best subserved by a choir of men and boys. While the trained boy voice is indisputably the most beautiful of all, the untrained boy voice is exactly the reverse. We have much better raw material in the voices of girls and young women. They **Advantages of the female voice.** naturally produce a more agreeable quality of tone, they are innately more refined and mu-

sical, and far better results can be obtained
from them with less ability and effort on the
part of the choirmaster, than is the case with
boys. Moreover they are better behaved, more
docile, and their voices have not the annoying
trick of breaking when the point of maximum
usefulness has been gained. It is a question
of relative values in many instances. On the
one hand we have the male choir with its traditional authority and fitness, plus coarse singing, poor interpretation, and boisterous behav-
iour; on the other we have the mixed choir with
its violation of churchly custom, plus better
voices, more artistic finish, and better conduct.

The writer would at once cast his vote for **Arrange-** **ment of** the latter, provided always that the girls or **mixed** **choir.** women were not permitted to sit in the chancel.
They could occupy seats in the front pews
where they would be sufficiently near the men
to produce a good effect musically. Academic
gowns and "mortar-board" caps would seem the
most appropriate garb for the women, while the
men (occupying the chancel) would retain their
historic vestments. This arrangement would
not interfere with the much-beloved choral pro-
cessionals, as the women could file into their
seats, the men diverging into the chancel.[2]

In some cases one-half of the frantic effort

---

[2] The processional is a purely American habit, and is
only indulged in on special occasions in England.

spent in sustaining an unsatisfactory boy choir would result in a good mixed choir, which would render the music in an agreeable and effective manner. Good results are also obtained with a few good women voices when the boys are weak and unequal to the task. One hears excellent music by choirs of this character, but unfortunately the unchurchly custom of seating the women in the chancel is generally followed.

The quartette choir. Even the quartette choir is not an unmitigated evil. If proper music is selected, and the voices are well-trained and agreeable, very good music is indeed possible, if not of the most desirable churchly quality. However, one good singer to lead the congregational singing, and to **The precentor.** do an occasional solo, is preferable to a poor quartette, and infinitely better than a combination of two or three voices when the harmony will be out of balance. The writer heard some **A choir of girls only.** quite satisfactory singing by a choir of but four girls in a Northern Michigan church. They were vested but occupied seats in the transept in front of the organ. The voices were fresh and good, and of ample volume to fill the small church. In the hands of an experienced organist very excellent music indeed could have been supplied by these four young girls. But there, again, is the crux of the whole situation, an experienced organist! Small towns do not possess them and small churches cannot afford to pay them. In any congregation of a hundred people there is hidden enough musical ability to make a good choir provided there is a musician at hand with sufficient wit, devotion, and resourcefulness to extract it. This is where England has a great advantage over us. Between her choir schools and her many fine choirs she is supplied with capable choirmasters who know their business, and their number is constantly increasing, but with us, outside of the large cities, capable choir leaders are indeed few and far between. Here again the necessity for the adequate training of church musicians is brought to the fore—a training which the Church herself should provide.

Limitations and possibilities of small parishes.

England's advantages and our deficiencies.

One of the greatest evils attending the boy choir in the small church is the spirit of misplaced emulation which seeks to use precisely the same music that is sung in the larger churches with well-equipped choirs. Nothing is more painful, reprehensible, or utterly inexcusable than the performance of music beyond the capacity of a choir. Man is not edified nor God glorified by a choir madly wrestling with music beyond its powers, offending sensitive ears with its unseemly noises, and keeping the auditors in a state of nervous tension for fear of a total collapse! The whole object and purpose of music is perverted under such circumstances.

Small choirs too ambitious.

Justice due the composer.

A composer gives forth to the world his best thoughts, assuming at least that they will be sung in tune and with reasonable accuracy, agreeable tone production, and intelligent interpretation—else his most noble conceptions become travesties and instead of offering to Almighty God something worthy of His praise, we offer Him but a caricature of what the composer intended.

Choirmaster to blame.

Choirmasters are principally to blame for this lamentable state of affairs, and it results from one of two causes: either the choirmaster is incapable of selecting music suited to the capacity of his forces, and hence must borrow ideas from his neighbors, or else he thinks that for the protection of his own dignity and standing he must have compositions of a certain class on his programmes, regardless of how they may be performed.

Choirs need incentive.

But the retort is made that you cannot interest a choir for any length of time by singing hymns and chants and simple anthems. There is a modicum of truth in this. Choirs, and especially volunteer choirs, must be kept interested or disintegration will set in. To a certain extent choristers must be kept on their mettle and be given tasks that require application and perseverance. To sing the same old things over and over again will demoralize any choir; they must have change and new incentives to effort.

To meet this necessity there is an enormous output of church music, of all degrees of merit and difficulty, and it is being added to every day at an astonishing rate. To select properly from this immense mass requires time, patience, experience, and judgment, qualities that are not often found in one choirmaster, especially if he is on scant pay. It is much simpler and easier to note the programmes of neighboring churches and to use these selections whether they are suitable or not.

Another factor in the equation is that choirmasters who have not the ability or knack of getting a good tone become dulled in their musical perceptions and take roughness and crudeness as a necessary evil that cannot be eliminated.

While it frequently is desirable to have a choir modify its ambitions respecting the use of difficult and intricate compositions, it is not intended to imply that there should be a weakening in the quality of the music selected. There is good and bad music from the simplest to the most complex. It is a fact that there is little difficulty in interesting the members of a choir in good music. They may object at the start, but with a little perseverance good music is sure to win its way. As with hymn singing, if good standards once prevail no inferior product will suffice. But it is equally to the point to cultivate the taste and perception of the singers as regards artistic, musical interpretation—to appreciate good tone quality, fine shading and expression, accuracy, and good pitch. Here, again, where the esthetic sensibilities have once been thoroughly aroused, nothing short of good work will satisfy the singers.

Boys and young men are prone to look upon singing as an athletic exercise for the display of strength. There is a certain excitement in making a noise, and this in addition to the mental alertness required in reading words and music at once, together with the pleasure in the music itself, makes rather an attractive occupation. So, unless carefully guided, the young idea is apt to acquire a very mistaken notion of what music really is. When once an appreciation of the "still small voice" is awakened and when a chorister can discriminate between mere noise and musical sonority, many of the choirmaster's troubles will have disappeared.

It is difficult, however, to establish these desirable conditions of esthetic advancement unless choristers have the advantage of daily drill in music, and daily drill is only possible when there is a choir school. This brings us back to the important subject of the choir school, the institution which has given to England its acknowledged preëminence over all other nations in the matter of musical services.

Although Trinity Church, New York City, does not maintain a choir school, it is in her records that we first find mention of attempts in that direction. The children of her charity school, established in 1709, were the first to receive instruction in church music, although it was of the most elementary character. Later the school became exclusively a boys' school. In 1843 steps were taken by the vestry of the parish to improve the musical instruction and, doubtless under pressure from Dr. Edward Hodges, the noted organist, sixteen scholarships were established for pupils of the parish school, who were to be instructed in music two days a week by the parish musical director. The scheme, however, did not prove very satisfactory, Dr. Hodges reporting in 1847 that "Trinity school does not furnish musical talent enough to feed the class." The boys at this period sat in the gallery opposite the altar and were not vested.

About the year 1870 in the Cathedral of SS. Peter and Paul, Chicago, a parish day school was in existence which was also intended to serve as a choir school. The resources of the Cathedral did not permit of the employment of a professional musician, and the instruction of the choristers in music was undertaken by

Canon Knowles. Daily choral morning and evening services were maintained until the great fire in 1871, when conditions were created which put an end to the venture, although both the Cathedral and the school buildings escaped the ravages of the flames.

The first church in this country to establish permanently a choir school was St. Paul's, Baltimore, where the venerable Dr. J. S. B. Hodges was rector. It is peculiarly appropriate that this should be the case, for Dr. Hodges is not only an accomplished musician but also a son of the famous Dr. Edward Hodges already referred to in connection with "Old Trinity," New York. St. Paul's choir school was founded in 1873 and accommodates thirty boys. A priest is headmaster with a musician as assistant. Two courses of study are offered, one leading to college, the other to holy orders, with the result that seven graduates have been ordained ministers of the Church.

The first choir school in New York City was established by Grace Church, Broadway and Tenth street. Grace Church was one of the last to abandon the quartette choir, but when it adopted the vested choir it did so in no half-hearted way, for liberal provision was made for the support and maintenance of the choristers. Some six years ago a splendidly equipped building was erected for the use of the choir school, containing reception room, library, diningroom, dormitories for sixteen boys, besides the necessary domestic quarters and an infirmary with apartments for trained nurses. An adjoining tower supplies lecture and recitation rooms, and a gymnasium. The roofs of both structures provide a playground after the manner of St. Paul's choir-house in London. Fourteen day scholars are accepted in addition to the sixteen boarders. The latter are attracted from all parts of the country by the superiority of the instruction, including as it does courses leading to a business as well as to a professional life, and by the distinction of singing in a prominent metropolitan church.

Business and professional courses.

A choir school was maintained at Fond du Lac, Wis., for some years, where the Cathedral Close is surrounded by a group of solidly-constructed buildings which are excellent models of good ecclesiastical architecture. The group includes the Cathedral proper (with its stained glass, its artistic frescoes, sculpture and paintings), a large and finely equipped Girls' School, a Clergy-house and a Choir School. Unfortunately, through lack of funds the latter is temporarily closed.

Cathedral Choir school, Fond du Lac.

The Cathedral of St. John the Divine in New York City, looking to the future establishment of a more complete plant, instituted a day school for choristers some years since.

Cathedral Choir school, New York City.

Like the school at Grace Church, the instruction offered is of such a nature as to draw a very desirable class of boys, while the gymnasium and military drill are additional attractions. Candidates for admission must be from nine to eleven years of age, of good character, and give promise of real vocal and musical ability. After acceptance they are periodically examined, and if found wanting musically or otherwise they are dropped from the rolls. Furthermore the parents are obliged to sign an agreement not to withdraw their sons from the school without express permission.

St. Thomas' Church, Fifth avenue, New York, is another instance of a parish slow to introduce the surpliced choir but ready to give generous support to the change the moment it is once decided upon. Five years ago this church maintained a famous musical service performed by a quartette and mixed chorus. It has funds in hand, it is reported, for the erection of a choir school and will doubtless be the next to provide itself with adequately trained boys.

The new Cathedral at Washington has plans already drawn for a magnificent choir school. A generous Churchwoman has made ample financial provision, not only for the building, but for an endowment as well. We therefore have promise in the near future of choirs that should vie with the best in England and which should be a constant incentive to the wealthier parishes to "go and do likewise."

Choir schools can be maintained at an expense varying from fifteen hundred dollars per annum to ten times that amount. The minimum sum would naturally represent a modest establishment for day scholars only, and it could support but a headmaster and one assistant. But with the right instruction and instructors such a school, with its close personal attention, its superior moral tone, and its musical advantages, would offer decided attractions. Such adjuncts as a gymnasium and military drill (which appeal so strongly to the boys themselves) would require a larger appropriation but would doubtless pay in the end. The proposition of housing and boarding students would call for still more funds and could only be considered by wealthy parishes.

It is quite within the range of possibility for a choir school to attain such a degree of excellence in its instruction, outside of the musical subjects, as to attract pay students in sufficient numbers to either partly or wholly defray the cost of maintenance.[3]

Expense of choir schools.

Possibility of self-maintenance.

---

[3] In addition to its Cathedrals, England has some thirty or forty parishes and college chapels supplied with choir schools. Magdalen College, Oxford, maintains its choir from an endowment left some five centuries ago. A condition of the bequest is to the effect that the support of the choir is the last thing to suffer in case of a shrinkage of income. In the more famous schools a notice of a vacancy brings

Choir schools the one satisfactory solution.

The choir school is the one satisfactory solution of the "boy choir" question, but unfortunately it is a solution open to comparatively few of our churches. The many parishes which could not possibly consider the establishment of such a school will have to content themselves with existing circumstances, in the hope that the near future may produce a larger supply of capable, reverent, and devoted Church musicians.

Literature on vested choirs.

The literature on the formation, the training, and the management of boy choirs is so plentiful, practical, and up-to-date that it would be a waste of time and effort to give any hints or suggestions along these lines in a paper of this nature. Excellent books are published on both sides of the Atlantic, but those bearing an American imprint will be found the more useful, as the conditions in this country are distinctly different from those in England.

Church choir training. John Troutbeck.

One of the oldest English books on the subject is by Dr. Troutbeck, a former precentor of Westminster Abbey. It gives a wholesome insight into what is expected of a thoroughly trained choir, and contains a valuable list of services and anthems for all possible occasions and of the highest merit. J. Varley Roberts in

---

a flood of applications, and all concerning boys of superior musical and general intelligence.

his "Practical Methods of Training Choristers" reveals the processes by which he has attained such superior results with his noted choir at Magdalen College, Oxford. It is admirably edited and printed and contains fifty-four pages of practical exercises. The "Art of Training Choir Boys," from the hands of Sir George Martin, organist and choirmaster of St. Paul's Cathedral, London, is a concise and useful book by that eminent Church musician and lays stress on the necessity of a knowledge of voice culture. It is supplied with copious vocal exercises.

A. Madeley Richardson, formerly organist and choirmaster at St. Saviour's Collegiate Church, London, has a very valuable book in his "Choir-Training Based on Voice Production." It covers the whole field of choir music and is written in an incisive and clear style. The same author's book on "Church Music" in Longmans, Green & Co.'s "Hand-books for the Clergy," takes up the whole question of Church music in a most interesting and vigorous manner. Richardson is a modern of the moderns, and his book will be especially enjoyed by those who have no sympathy with Gregorian chants, plainsong hymn tunes, or Palestrina motettes, subjects which he treats with scant courtesy.

J. S. Spencer Curwen, the great "tonic sol-

"The Boy Voice." J. S. S. Curwen.

faist," has a book entitled "The Boy Voice" which is sort of a compendium on the subject, as it has contributions from a number of noted choirmasters.   In this country the most widely known and popular book is "Hints on Boy-Choir Training," by Dr. G. E. Stubbs, organist and choirmaster of St. Agnes' Chapel, Trinity Parish, New York. Dr. Stubbs is one of the best known and best equipped writers on Church music and has charge of the Ecclesiastical Department of the "New Music Review." His book is eminently practical and displays a thorough knowledge of our needs in boy-choir training.   The book has passed through several editions.

A more recent work and one also capitally adapted to the American boy in the American Church is "In the Choir-room," by Walter Henry Hall, organist and choirmaster of the Cathedral of St. John the Divine, New York City.   Like all true choir trainers, Mr. Hall is a specialist in tone production, and he gives many practical directions in developing the boy voice.

"Clergy and Choir," by the Rev. Charles R. Hodge of New Lenox, Ill., is a book of rather more extended scope as it also considers congregational singing, mixed choirs, quartette choirs, children's music, the organ, the organist, etc.   It is interesting and gives the clergy-man's point of view.

"Choralia," by the Rev. James Baden Powell, is a most readable and suggestive book by the precentor of St. Paul's, Knightsbridge, London, where he has established a parochial service noted for its beauty and dignity.   Like Richardson's "Church Music" it deals with the question of ecclesiastical music at large and is not essentially a manual on choir-training.

While this bibliography[4] of the subject of vested choirs is not complete, it is at least suf-ficient to show that the subject has received careful attention at the hands of skilled spe-cialists, and that no one interested need remain in ignorance regarding the most approved meth-ods of forming and developing boy choirs.   But it is astonishing how uninformed the average choirmaster is concerning his own business, and how he prefers his own happy-go-lucky methods rather than to profit by the experience and sug-gestions of men who have made a pronounced success of their work.   The subject is important enough to demand most careful thought and study both on the part of the priest and the choirmaster.

---

[4] For additional works on Vested Choirs see Bibliography in the Appendix.

VI.

THE DEVELOPMENT OF MUSIC IN THE ANGLICAN CHURCH.

Plainsong an artistic product.

It is not generally known, even among people interested in music, that a highly developed system of Church music existed before the twelfth century, a system not only complete and perfect in itself, but capable of great expressiveness. Moreover it is the only system that has ever been formally adopted by the Church and prescribed as the authentic musical setting to its Liturgy. Yet this is the case and the so-called "plainsong" of the early Church, far from being the crude beginnings of modern music, or a worn-out and discarded art form, remains to-day a complete entity in itself, full of vital force and meaning to those who seriously study and adequately comprehend it.

Origin of plainsong.

The Liturgy of the Church was originally conceived for musical expression and was always intended to be sung. It appropriated the musical idiom of its day and generation, an idiom derived from the complicated system of Greek scales with perhaps traces of the traditional Temple music of the Hebrews. Out of this material grew the system variously known as plainsong, plain chant, Gregorian chant, or Gregorian tones. As has been already stated, the Greek scales or modes which formed the basis of plainsong were originally four in number: the Dorian, the Phrygian, the Lydian, and the Mixo-Lydian. These scales correspond to a conjunct series of white notes on the piano beginning with D, E, F, and G, respectively. If a melody confined itself to any one of these scales and did not exceed its keynote more than one adjacent note at either end, it was in the "authentic" mode of its series. For example, AMERICA is an authentic mode for its melody lies within the octave of its keynote with the exception of the fourth note, which is immediately below the key note or "final." Later four collateral or "plagal" modes were developed, each of which was founded upon an authentic scale but began and ended a fourth lower but retained the same "final" as the scale from which it was derived. Thus OLD HUNDRED is in a plagal mode, for its range extends four notes below and five notes above its "final," the latter appearing as the central note of the melody, rather than its highest or lowest note. Tradition ascribes the authentic modes to St. Ambrose and the plagal modes to St. Gregory. In any event St. Gregory collected

The Greek scales.
Authentic modes.
Plagal modes.
St. Ambrose.
St. Gregory.

The Anti-phonarium.

the various chants then in use, systematized them in an authoritative volume called the "Antiphonarium," and established singing schools for instruction in their proper performance. Thus his name became inseparably connected with plainsong chants.[1]

Present major and minor scales the last to be developed.

Our modern major and minor scales appeared later in two additional modes known as the Ionian and the Æolian, respectively. AMERICA is thus Ionian and OLD HUNDRED Hypo-Ionian. The plainsong tune to "Come, Holy Ghost, our souls inspire" is Mixo-Lydian, while "O come, O come, Emmanuel" is Dorian.[2]

Gregorian chants but small part of plain-song.

The Gregorian chants as known in the Anglican Church are but a very small part of the plainsong system. Their use is confined to the psalms and canticles. There are in addition most elaborate settings of the usual Mass numbers as well as for the variable Introits, Graduales, Offertories, Sequences, etc. Each

---

[1] The plagal modes received the prefix "hypo." Consequently the Hypo-Dorian scale began on A but had its final on D; the Hypo-Phrygian on B with its final on E, etc. If *America* is played beginning on D and nothing but the white notes employed, it will be in the authentic Dorian mode. If the same process is pursued with *Old Hundred* the plagal Hypo-Dorian mode will result. If the same tunes are begun in E. the two Phrygian modes will be heard, if on F the two Lydian, if on G the two Mixo-Lydian. It must not be forgotten that the white notes are alone to be played. Experiments with these well-known melodies will at once impress the listener with the radical difference between the modern major scale and the ancient ecclesiastical modes.

[2] This latter melody is really Æolian, but the Dorian mode was later modified by lowering the sixth note of the, scale, which made it agree with the Æolian in the order of its steps and half-steps.

Mass number had its proper mode, but the tune varied for the different Church seasons.[3] It is claimed that to have a command of plainsong melodies for all the offices of the Roman Church one must know at least a thousand tunes, no two of which are exactly alike. Many of these melodies are of great charm and beauty and owe much of their attractiveness to the habit of singing melodic phrases to a single syllable. These groups of notes were known variously as ligatures, perieleses, melismas, or jubilations. A German writer thus comments upon the inner essence of this ancient art:

Peculiarities of plainsong.

> "In the Middle Ages nothing was known of accompaniment; there was not the slightest need of one. The substance of the musical content, which we to-day commit to interpretation through harmony, the old musicians laid on melody. The latter accomplished in itself the complete utterance of the artistically-aroused fantasy. In this particular the melismas, which carry the extensions of the tones of the melody, are a necessary means of presentation in medieval art; they proceed logically out of the principles of the unison melody. Text repetition is

No need of accompaniment.

Melismas.

---

[3] The following names were given to the eight original Gregorian modes as indicative of their esthetic content:
First Mode (Dorian) "Modus Gravis."
Second Mode (Hypo-Dorian) "Modus Tristis."
Third Mode (Phrygian) "Modus Mysticus."
Fourth Mode (Hypo-Phrygian) "Modus Harmonicus."
Fifth Mode (Lydian) "Modus Laetus."
Sixth Mode (Hypo-Lydian) "Modus Devotus."
Seventh Mode (Mixo-Lydian) "Modus Angelicus."
Eighth Mode (Hypo-Mixo-Lydian) "Modus Perfectus."

unknown. While modern singers repeat an especially emphatic thought or word, the old melodists repeat a melody or phrase which expresses the ground mood of the texts in a striking manner. And they not only repeat it, but they make it unfold, and draw out of it new tones of melody. This method is certainly not less artistic than the later text repetition, it comes nearer, also, to the natural expression of the devotionally inspired heart."

Pneumae.

Not only were the melismas referred to in the above quotation employed, but echoing phrases to inarticulate sounds were added called pneumae. These ornate phrases are extremely difficult to sing and require long training. Schools were established as early as the fourth century under St. Sylvester, and certain monasteries, notably that at St. Gall, Switzerland, were noted for their expertness both in singing and teaching this difficult art.

Plainsong in England. St. Augustine (596).

This was the musical system that St. Augustine carried to England in the year 596 at the behest of Gregory the Great, although he was cautioned not to insist upon the Roman use should it be objected to in the older British churches. However, it was adopted by York and Canterbury and soon spread to other localities. As was the case on the continent, the authentic melodies as found in the Antiphonarium established by Gregory became corrupted and many local "uses" came into vogue. Of

The marginal note "No text repetition." appears beside the first paragraph; "Adopted by York and Canterbury." appears beside the last paragraph.

these the Sarum or Salisbury Use was of great **Sarum Use.**
beauty despite its unauthenticity, and later
was considered as a model for Anglican
churches. As soon as Roman supremacy was
thrown off and the use of the Latin tongue dispensed with, the ancient plainsong was adapted
to the vernacular. The first part of the Eng-
lish service to appear in print was the Litany, **Cranmer's Litany.**
translated by Archbishop Cranmer and ar-
ranged to its traditional plainsong melody.
This was in 1544. In 1550 John Merbecke **John Merbecke (1550).**
(or Marbecke) published his famous "Booke of
Common Praier Noted," which was an adaptation of the plainsong of the earlier rituals to
the first liturgy of Edward VI. Bumpus in
his "English Cathedral Music" thus speaks of
the work:

> "This, the earliest choral book our Church
> possesses, was not merely a Directory for the
> performance of Matins and Evensong, but it
> also contained the office of the Holy Communion
> and that of the Burial of the Dead. It was
> noted throughout for priest and people. Thus
> it supplied a deficiency sure to be felt through-
> out the country on the substitution of the Eng-
> lish for the Latin rite. It is not easy to dis-
> cover the precise extent to which Merbecke's
> book was used in the English Cathedral service
> during the latter half of the sixteenth century.
> Primarily intended for the use of the Chapel
> Royal, it constituted a model for the whole coun-
> try, and its adoption as the authentic choral

book of the Church—not only for choirs, but also for congregations—is placed beyond all doubt. Based musically upon the Use of Sarum, it formed a complete ' antiphonarium' for the reformed liturgy."

This first edition of Merbecke was not harmonized, the plainsong being alone printed on the old four-line stave. In 1844 William Pickering of London printed a beautiful facsimile with its rubricated staves, diamond-headed notes, black-letter type, and ample margins.

Merbecke's the standard plainsong service. Merbecke's adaptation of the plainsong to the English text was done so thoroughly and well that it has remained to this day unchanged and has always been the standard plainsong service. In recent years both John Stainer and **Harmonized versions.** Basil Harwood have edited Merbecke with harmonies, and its sturdy, manly music is winning the recognition it deserves. The Nicene Creed is especially fine and is particularly suitable for Advent and Lent.

Beginnings of part writing. In the meantime the art of counterpoint and of harmony had made considerable advancement. Composers sought to put several melodies together and in course of time masses appeared in two, four, six, eight, twelve and even in forty parts, some of them masterpieces of musical ingenuity, far surpassing in this respect the efforts of modern writers.

At times composers would develop the music for the entire mass from a single plainsong melody or *cantus firmus,* as it was called. In this case the mass would take its name from the melody in question and we would have the *Missa, "Veni, Sponsa Christi," "Tu es Petrus,"* etc., as the case might be. Occasionally the musical subject would be borrowed from secular sources, and not always of the most commendable nature. Thus we have the mass of the "Armed Man" and the mass of the "Red Noses."

In 1560 a book was published by John Day with the following title:

> "Certaine Notes set forthe in foure and three partes, to be song at Mornyng, Communion, and Evenyng Praier, very necessarie for the Church of Christe to be frequented and used: and unto them be added divers Godly Praiers and psalms in the like forme to the honour and prayse of God. Imprinted at London, over Aldersgate, beneath St. Martin's, by John Day."

These compositions were in the contrapuntal style, a style which is of far more artistic merit than the ordinary church music of today. Instead of a pleasing melody in the soprano to which the other parts supply agreeable harmonies, the contrapuntal style endeavors to have each voice part of equal importance and melodic beauty, so that we have a combination of independent melodies, harmonizing with each other and welded into a complete whole. This style of music was also supplied to the Motette, which later developed into the Anthem.[4]

Thomas Tallis (1520-1585).

To this period belongs Thomas Tallis, the first English Church composer of note. He is known principally by his Versicles and Responses and his Litany, which are in general use to-day throughout the Anglican communion. It is to be hoped that their devout and churchly strains may never cease, for they link us directly with the earliest days of our Prayer Book and lay stress upon our historic continuity.

Tallis' Responses.

Tallis made use of the traditional plainsong melodies in his Versicles and Responses and harmonized them in a masterful manner. It is a matter of dispute whether the harmonization was originally in four or five parts. In this country we are accustomed to a four part version while in England they are generally sung in five parts.[5]

Tallis' great gifts as a composer.

Tallis' reputation as the greatest composer

---

[4] The term Motette was first confined to unaccompanied sacred music with Latin text, the latter being neither a canticle or a Mass number.

[5] While on the subject of the choral service it might be added that unless a priest is available who can sing his part in an acceptable manner, it is best dispensed with. If the intoning is out of tune or performed inaccurately or inadequately it is distressing in the extreme. To have the priest's part read and the responses sung is equally reprehensible. It is but patchwork at best and serves no purpose whatever.

of his day, however, does not rest upon his harmonization of the responses, but upon a large number of masses, motettes, and anthems, compositions that are preëminently musical and scholarly and which command the respect of musicians of all time. Like most musicians of that epoch, Tallis changed his religion to suit that of the Crown, writing with equal facility masses and motettes for the Roman service or communion services and anthems for the Anglican. But as he largely favored the Latin text it would seem that at heart he was a Roman Catholic. The most remarkable specimen of Tallis' contrapuntal skill is his "Song in Forty Parts," which was written for eight choirs of five parts each. Davey in his "History of English Music" comments as follows upon this extraordinary *tour de force*:

Tallis' Song in forty parts.

> "Every earnest student should thoroughly examine this work, noting how the themes are fugued through the choirs, how the various sections of the great choral body are employed antiphonally, how long-sustained harmonies are occasionally varied by quickly changing successions of chords, and how imposing an effect is produced by the two rests for all the voices, especially the one before the last clause, when thirteen of the voices stop in the chord of C, and, after a minim rest, all the forty enter on the chord of A. Everything an unaccompanied choir can do is required in this masterpiece of the polyphonic style."

Richard Farrant (circa 1564).

Richard Farrant was a contemporary of Tallis and a man of real talent. Several of his anthems are still in use in the English Cathedrals, and are sung occasionally in this country. The anthem, "Lord, for Thy tender mercies' sake," is the most popular, but its authenticity is seriously questioned—experts assigning it to a much later period than the middle of the sixteenth century.

Venetian tribute to English music.

A Venetian ambassador at the Court of Henry VIII. wrote as follows concerning English Church music at this period: "The mass was sung by His Majesty's choristers, whose voices were more divine than human. They did not chant like men, but gave praise like angels."

Thus early was the supremacy of Anglican art recognized and acknowledged.

William Byrd (1558-1623).

William Byrd and Orlando Gibbons were worthy successors to Tallis and Farrant and they added greatly to the fame of English music. Byrd, who was a Roman Catholic, wrote mostly to Latin texts and many of his motettes have since been arranged to English words. He left a legacy of fifty-four anthems and the following quaint defence of the art of singing:

> 1. It is a knowledge easily taught and quickly learned, where there is a good master and an apt scoller.
> 2. The exercise of singing is delightful to nature, and good to preserve the health of man.

3. It doth strengthen all parts of the breast and doth open the pipes.

4. It is a singular good remedie for a stuttering and stammering in the speech.

5. It is the best means to procure a perfect pronunciation and to make a good orator.

6. It is the only way to find out where nature hath bestowed the benefit of a good voice.

7. Because there is no music of instruments whatever to be compared to the voyces of men, when they are good, well-sorted, and ordered.

8. The better the voyce, the meeter it is to honour and serve God therewith, and the voyce of man is chiefly to be employed to that end.

"Since singing is so good a thing
I wish all men would learn to sing."

Orlando Gibbons is considered one of the best of England's musicians, and he is frequently referred to as the English Palestrina. Like Byrd, he wrote many madrigals, but there was little distinction made between the sacred and secular styles in those days beyond the text. With Gibbons, who was a Protestant, the habit of writing to Latin texts largely disappeared, and a new era in church music set in which is best explained by the following quotation:

Orlando Gibbons (1583-1625).

"Gibbons, as it were, stood at the parting of the ways. Brought up with the strains of Tallis, Byrd, Tye, Merbecke, and other worthies of the old school ringing in his ears, he perceived that another world of music was opening: emotion and expression were destined to take the place of orderly, though cold, counterpoint. This new feeling is reflected in his music, sacred and secular. On this foundation Gibbons built up a series of noble anthems, different from anything that had appeared before his time. It is exalted music that flows along with a stately melody, grand in its sonorous harmony, and impressive in its religious solemnity."

The Festival of the Three Choirs, which comprises the Cathedral choirs of Gloucester, Worcester and Hereford, frequently makes use of Gibbons' fine anthems to this day, and this is true of a number of other important musical gatherings.[6]

Decline of music during the Commonwealth. The flourishing condition of English Church music suffered a serious decline during the troublous times of Charles I. and of the Commonwealth under Cromwell. Political and religious dissensions were not congenial to the gentler arts, and many composers of music forsook the pen for the sword. Under the fanaticism of the Puritans the stately Cathedrals were disfigured and despoiled, organs and val-

---

[6] There was a curious custom in those days of collecting "spur money" from any person entering a Cathedral wearing spurs. Their jangling was supposed to interrupt the service and choir-boys were permitted to extort a small fee from any and all offenders. Even the King was not exempt from it as entries in the the royal expense account prove. The boys, doubtless to the detriment of their vocal efforts, were constantly on the lookout for victims, and never allowed them to escape. On one occasion the boys made way with a recalcitrant's hat, and on complaint to a magistrate the boys were sustained in their traditional rights. In some places the victim had the right to demand that the youngest of the boys sing his "gamut"—a somewhat complicated form of scale. Upon failure no "spur money" could be collected. This custom obtained as late as 1850 in some of the Cathedrals.

uable collections of music representing the accumulation of many years were destroyed, and the singing of music other than that of the metrical psalms was prohibited. In the short space of fifteen years the traditions for the performance of the choral service were all but lost. It took some time to restore the Cathedral service to its former standard of excellence and there was a lack of uniformity in the various dioceses. The "uses" were at such variance that it was thought necessary to have a standard version established. At the request of the University of Oxford Edward Lowe compiled a manual in 1661 entitled "'A Short Direction for the Performance of Cathedral Service,' publisht for the information of such persons who are ignorant of it, and shall be called to officiate in Cathedral and Collegiate Churches, where it hath formerly been in use."

Edward Lowe's Cathedral Service (1661).

This Directory contained the responses and litany as noted by Cranmer and Merbecke; two settings for the Te Deum to a chant known as "Canterbury tune" (one for men's voices and the other in four-part harmony), Festival responses and Litany by Tallis, and a hymn.

The Restoration found no boys capable of taking their parts in the Cathedral services. We read that

Dearth of boys.

> "for above a year after the opening of His Majesty's Chapell, the orderers of the Musick

there were necessitated to supply superior parts of the music with cornets, and men's feigned voices, there being not one lad for all that time capable of singing his part readily."[7]

Church music under Charles II.

Under the influence of Charles II. music underwent a change which at the time could be hardly called for the better, but which eventually proved advantageous. The King had become accustomed to the French style of music during his exile, and Tudway, the historian, thus comments upon the then state of affairs:

"The standard of Church music began by Mr. Tallis, Mr. Byrd, etc., was continued for some years after ye Restauration, and all Composers conformed themselves to ye Pattern which was set by them. His Majesty, who was a brisk and airy prince, coming to ye crown in ye flower and vigor of his age, was soon, if I may say so, tyred with ye grave and solemn ways, and ordered ye Composers of his Chapel to add symphonys, etc., with instruments to their anthems, and thereupon established a select number of his private musick to play ye symphonys and Ritornelles which he had appointed. The king did not intend by this innovation to alter anything of the established way. He only appointed this to be done when he came himself to ye chappell which was only upon Sundays, on ye mornings of ye great Festivals and Days of Offerings. The old masters, viz., Dr. Child,

---

[7] The cornet was a reed instrument somewhat like the oboe, though coarser in tone, and not the familiar brass band instrument of the present day. They were often made of wood covered with leather. Under these conditions composers were constrained to write music for men's voices alone until boys could be properly trained.

Dr. Gibbons, and Mr. Lowe, organists to His Majesty, hardly knew how to comport themselves with these new-fangled ways, but proceeded in their compositions according to ye old style, and therefore there are only some full services and anthems of theirs to be found."

A Captain Henry Cook was made master of the children of the Chapel Royal after the Restoration and soon succeeded in gathering together a remarkably gifted set of young choristers, some of whom developed into the greatest musicians of their day. One of the most talented was Pelham Humphreys. His abilities so attracted the attention of the King that he was sent to Paris to study with the great Lulli, the most famous of the early French composers. Humphreys, who was but twenty when he returned from an extended stay in Paris, brought back with him a touch of the French style. He introduced the declamatory recitative, an Italian device, into English church music, and also added new harmonies to the English stock in trade. John Blow was another of Captain Cook's famous boys who developed into a good composer. In the music both of Humphreys and Blow the element of the picturesque and dramatic came more to the fore and the texts to their anthems were evidently chosen with these qualities in view.

The anthems of the earlier composers, taking

their pattern from the Latin motette, were for the full choir from beginning to end, and if accompanied by the organ, the latter simply duplicated the voice parts. The taste of the King led to a freer treatment of the organ part, and preludes and interludes were added. The next development was the breaking up of the full anthem into contrasting sections for one, two or more parts, to be sung either by solo voices or more usually by one side of the choir. This was known as the "Verse Anthem" in contradiction to the "Full Anthem." The organ was necessarily an integral part of the Verse Anthem for it supplied the verse parts with proper accompaniment, especially when there were not sufficient parts to complete the harmony. The instruments used in addition to the organ were the violins, the cornets or oboes, and the sackbuts or trombones.

The Verse Anthem.

Dr. John Blow had one pupil of such preeminent abilities that he requested to have the fact that he was "Master to the famous Mr. Henry Purcell" engraved upon his tombstone. And it is further stated that he resigned his position as organist of Westminster Abbey that this young man, then twenty-two, might have the post. Henry Purcell was not only the greatest of English composers but the greatest musician of his age, not excepting Lulli in France or Scarlatti in Italy. Germany had not

Henry Purcell (1658-1695)

Greatest musician of his age.

as yet produced a really great composer, as the mighty Johann Sebastian Bach was not born until 1685, twenty-seven years after Purcell's birth.

Purcell was also one of Captain Cook's boys, and upon his death Purcell came under the charge of Pelham Humphreys, and upon the demise of that talented man at the early age of twenty-seven, Dr. Blow became his master. Purcell wrote no less than 107 anthems (besides many services and much secular music), works full of strength, dignity, breadth, and expressiveness. He brought to perfection the "verse" or "solo" anthem. He had no sympathy with the French tastes of the King and declared himself

> "to lean towards a just imitation of the most famous Italian masters, principally to bring the seriousness and gravity of that sort of music into vogue and reputation amongst our countrymen, whose humours it is time now should begin to loathe the levity and balladry of our neighbours, the French."

None of Purcell's music was published during his lifetime and his great gifts were but little appreciated. In fact up to 1828, when Vincent Novello began to publish four quarto volumes of Purcell's music, but a dozen anthems were known to exist in print. In 1836 a body of professional and amateur musicians formed a Purcell Club to study and perform his works.

This club gave annually at Westminster Abbey a morning and an afternoon service devoted to Purcell's works, and, after a dinner, a performance of his secular compositions in the evening. These meetings reached their climax in 1858, the bicentenary of Purcell's birth, when a grand commemoration was held, attended by a vast number of musicians and others.

Purcell developed the bass solo to its fullest dignity and in his verse anthems he treats the chorus parts with unusual brevity, but they are none the less effective in their grandeur and straightforwardness. Purcell died at the early age of thirty-seven and was interred at Westminster together with Tallis, Gibbons, Blow and other musical worthies. A critic in 1848 thus speaks of the Purcell celebration that year:

> "But what we remark with the greatest pleasure is the strong and growing passion of the public for his works. The immense crowd of hearers which filled all the open avenues of the Abbey, exhibiting the deepest interest in the music, afforded testimony to the progress of a composer who has not yet resumed his true position. The latest in this respect is the greatest. Every year's experience tends to show that Handel must ultimately make way for Purcell, and that the German history of vocal music, sacred and secular, needs certain corrections in favour of England."

The developments of sixty years have hardly borne out the hopes expressed by the above writer as far as popular appreciation is concerned, but Purcell still is held in the highest esteem by all earnest students of Church music.

After Purcell, who died in 1695, there was a gradual decline in the quality of English church compositions. William Croft, to whom the well-known hymn-tune St. Anne is attributed, was, however, a man of much force and left a list of nearly 100 anthems behind him. Croft was also a pupil of Dr. Blow's and well schooled in the dignified Cathedral style of writing. His compositions are still popular in the English Cathedrals, and Sir John Stainer pays the following tribute to his morning service in the key of A.

> "One of the finest, if not the finest, settings of the *Te Deum* and *Jubilate* to which the English Church can point is that by Croft in A. It combines a suitable variety of sentiment with a dignified unity as a whole; and while in turn it is plaintive, penitential, or joyous, it bursts at the close of the *Gloria* to the *Jubilate* into a rich Fugato, highly artistic and effective."

Croft also wrote a fine setting to the musical portions of the burial service which has been in constant use both in St. Paul's and the Abbey.

We now arrive at the time when Handel came to England. Owing to the fact that Handel spent the larger part of his artistic career in England and that he became a naturalized citizen in 1726 he is almost claimed as an English composer. It is unnecessary to enlarge upon the abilities of this great genius, upon the sublime qualities of his oratorios, or upon the commanding position he assumed among English musicians. He so towered above his contemporaries that their efforts seem weak and puny in comparison. While capellmeister to the Duke of Chandos he wrote twelve anthems on a grand scale, with orchestral accompaniment, known as the Chandos anthems, but his oratorios have attained such popularity that little attention is paid nowadays to his other works.

Chandos anthems.

The Rev. William Mason, Precentor of York Minster, thus criticised one of the Chandos anthems in 1782:

Early criticisms of Handel.

> "Mr. Handell has taken more liberty with the words than is usually done. So much indeed as might lead one to conclude that he formed the composition out of his musical commonplace, and adapted words to airs previously invented, which it is probable enough was the case, not only in this, but in many of his later productions."

This criticism is not without warrant, for Handel not only transferred themes of his own from instrumental pieces or operas to his sacred works but he appropriated material from other composers without the slightest compunction. However, it must be admitted that he developed

Handel's plagiarisms.

these stolen ideas in a marvelous manner and thus rescued them from oblivion. Another subject of criticism was his use of the orchestra, that he sacrificed the voices and melodic charm for the sake of instrumental effects. This criticism has a familiar sound, for the same fault has been found with Beethoven and Wagner, and it will continue to be found by those who look upon the orchestra as a mere accompaniment to the voices and not an added means for intensifying the general effect.

A great admirer and friend of Handel's was Dr. Maurice Greene, organist of St. Paul's Cathedral. Handel would frequently attend the afternoon service and after it was over he and Greene would lock themselves up in the church and Handel, stripped to his shirt, would play long into the evening on the fine organ built by the famous Father Smith. The organ contained a set of pedals, a rarity at that time.

Maurice Greene (1696-1755).

Greene composed anthems of no little merit, adding a touch of the German and Italian manner. Being a man of independent means, he had an ambition to collect and publish in full score the finest specimens of English Cathedral music, much of which was only in manuscript and sometimes only in separate voice parts. He did not live to complete his task, but turned over his material to Dr. William Boyce, who

Greene's anthems.

Boyce's Collection of English Cathedral Music. William Boyce (1710-1779)

published three notable volumes between the years 1760 and 1768.

Boyce also wrote good anthems, one especially, "O, where shall wisdom be found?" being still considered a very fine specimen of the Cathedral style. Boyce died in 1779 and for a period of about forty years after that date Church music rapidly deteriorated. It was in the days of the fox-hunting parsons, when religious life was at low ebb and those in authority took little or no interest in music and made no provision for its proper maintenance. As a consequence the dignified and stately music of the Cathedral school was neglected and the new compositions were of a florid and frivolous type, utterly out of harmony with a dignified and reverent service.

A craze for adaptations and arrangements set in. An ingenious Mr. Bond took excerpts from various works of Handel's, fitted them to new texts and called the patchwork an anthem. Worse still, passages from various composers of different nationalities would be worked over into a hodgepodge, and words were fitted to the music in the most careless manner. Italy had fallen from its high estate when Palestrina wrote his marvelous motettes and masses, and Italian composers with their ear-tickling and sensuous melodies became immensely popular in England. The masses of the Roman Church were drawn upon, not to be used in translation in the Communion service, but set to translations utterly at variance with the original text. Masses were written, and by composers of great fame, simply as show pieces of music and with little or no regard to the sacredness of the words.

But it was not long before the music of Haydn, Mozart, Beethoven, and Schubert, and, a little later, that of Schumann, Chopin, and Mendelssohn became known in England, and this knowledge brought new elements into English musical life. The effectiveness of music had gained enormously through the use of new and bolder harmonies, greater varieties of rhythm, and more complex processes of development. The spinet and clavichord evolved into the harpsichord, and that in turn into the pianoforte. Organs were immensely improved, both tonally and mechanically. The modern orchestra, developed from crude beginnings, arrived at a high state of development. Virtuosi, both vocal and instrumental, astounded the world with their marvelous gifts. The Cathedral style with its austere, classic dignity and impassive grandeur was to gain a richer and warmer color and to speak in more impassioned accents.

Thomas Atwood was the first English composer to be materially influenced by these changing conditions and he was also the first composer to attempt to drag England out of its musical slough of despond. In 1783 he went to Naples, studying with a local teacher. Two years later he went to Vienna, where he was the pupil and the close friend of Mozart. This graceful and poetic master's influence is plainly discernible in Atwood's music, for it is noticeable for its clearness and delicacy of taste.

Mozart's influence.

Felix Mendelssohn-Bartholdy (1809-1847).

Later Atwood became an intimate friend of Mendelssohn, the latter spending some time in Atwood's home in the suburbs of London, while recovering from an accident. Atwood was organist at St. Paul's and Mendelssohn, like Handel before him, was a great admirer of the Father Smith organ and would spend many hours improvising on this magnificent instrument, playing until the bellows blowers revolted.

Thomas Atwood Walmisley (1814-1856).

Of a more vigorous talent than Thomas Atwood's was that of his god-son, Thomas Atwood Walmisley, a composer who combined the dignity of the old school with the freedom of the new. A Magnificat and Nunc Dimittis of his in D minor is well known on both sides of the Atlantic and the somewhat sombre but fine setting is especially suitable for Advent or Lent.

The name of Wesley is quite as prominent in the musical history of England as it is in its religious history. Charles Wesley, the great hymn writer, had in the person of Samuel Wesley a wonderfully gifted son. He was born in 1766 and at the age of four he could play and improvise on the organ. He taught himself to read and write at the age of five by his unremitting study of Handel's oratorio of Samson, all of which he committed to memory. Before he was eight he wrote an oratorio which he called Ruth, and he presented the same to Dr. Boyce. Before he was of age he was a fine classical scholar, a splendid organist and pianist, and the most brilliant extempore player in England. Wesley wrote much for the Roman Catholic service and was thought to be in sympathy with it in his religious beliefs. This he denied, claiming only a musical interest in the matter. He was extremely fond of Gregorian music and said the greatest treat of his life was playing at a Gregorian Requiem when fifty priests sang the plainsong while he improvised the harmonies. Both as composer and performer Wesley ranked far above his contemporaries as well on the continent as in England. One of his sons, Samuel Sebastian Wesley, inherited his father's talent and worthily upheld his reputation. At the age of seven he became a chorister in the Chapel Royal under Hawes, who declared him to be the best boy who ever passed through his hands. Despite his talents (which received general recognition), he had a troubled

Samuel Wesley (1766-1837).

Wesley's precocity.

Brilliant extempore player.

High rank as player and composer.

Samuel Sebastian Wesley (1810-1876).

life, for the church authorities where he was engaged cared but little for music and gave Wesley scant opportunity to exercise his gifts. Although he had several Cathedral positions, it was only while he was organist at Leeds Parish Church that he received substantial and sympathetic support. Like his father, he was a famous organist, and very gifted in improvisation. *Solid style of organ playing.* He set the pattern for a solid, noble style of organ playing that has since placed England in the forefront as a country of fine organists. As a composer of sacred music he ranked with Spohr and Mendelssohn, and his anthem "The Wilderness" is considered a model in all respects. *Gifts as a composer.* To a greater extent than Atwood, his music shows the influence of continental music, and the severity of the Cathedral style is tempered by warmth of feeling and a picturesque imagination. Dr. Sparks, the well-known organist, thus speaks of the first performance of "The Wilderness":

> "Well do I remember the first rehearsal by the Exeter choir of *The Wilderness,* the astonishment and delight of the vicars choral with its rich and wonderful modulations, its deep religious fervor, its difficulties and grand effects. As one of the choir boys taking part in the lovely quartette at the end, 'And sorrow and sighing shall flee away,' I was greatly interested, and remember to this day the deep emotion which this inspiration awoke in me. If

possible, a still greater delight was afforded the choristers when they were taught to sing the fresh, responsive duet, 'See that ye love one another,' which forms part of the fine anthem 'Blessed be the God and Father.' "

This last mentioned work was written when internal troubles in the Church left Wesley with but one bass singer and the boys for Sunday duty, and for this sadly unbalanced collection of voices he wrote an anthem full of force and beauty.

With the Wesleys English Church music recovered from its lethargy and since that time England has had an unbroken chain of fine church composers, men of splendid technical equipment, of reverent attitude toward their work, and of expressive artistic powers. John Goss nobly upheld the new school of writing and enriched the stock of anthems with many fine specimens. His setting of "The Wilderness" vies with Wesley's in popularity and power, and his little anthem, "O Saviour of the world," has touched a multitude of hearts with its quiet beauty and deep religious feeling. Of similar calibre was Henry Smart, whose sterling service in F has found universal acceptance by reason of its honest, solid, and effective qualities. The Te Deum from this service is perhaps more widely used than any other setting. Macfarren, Sterndale Bennett, and Elvey are

Rise of Church music.

John Goss (1800-1880).

Henry Smart (1813-1879).

George Alexander Macfarren (1813-1887).

William Sterndale Bennett (1816-1875).

George Job Elvey (1816-1893).

other writers of this school and they each possess good, if not preëminent, qualities.

We now reach two very prominent names of modern times and their possessors have each had a widespread influence, although their styles are very different. The names are Joseph Barnby and John Stainer. In the lecture on hymn tunes the relative abilities and the characteristics of these two men were dwelt upon

Joseph Barnby (1838-1896).

at some length. Barnby strenuously objected to model his work after that of his predecessors and claimed the right to express his thoughts in his own idiom, unhampered by tradition. This he did in a striking way and his hymns, anthems, and services soon won immense popularity, although they were severely criticised by the more conservative members of the profession. Barnby delights in rich chromatic har-

Characteristics.

monies and in his choral works he borrows from the modern German part-song and the romantic school of instrumental music. There is a sensuous beauty about his compositions and a glow of color that is very fascinating, and when one is under the spell of it, it is difficult to judge aright of its real value. But Barnby has the faults of his virtues and his excessive use of harmonic color is more or less at the expense of solidity and real wearing qualities. His music is at times almost cloying in its richness, but despite this fact we would be loth to part with most of his music, for many of his compositions are of unquestionable worth.

Stainer represents qualities of a different type. While by no means imitative, his music in a manner is a logical evolution from that of the Wesleys, Goss, and Smart. It is essentially sane, solid and well-balanced, and at the same time it is full of imagination and expressiveness. He was particularly happy in selecting graphic texts and used plenty of words, thus avoiding vain repetitions—a glaring fault in some of his predecessors. One always feels the note of sincerity in his music, and the earnest desire to enhance the meaning of the text and the avoidance of effect for the mere sake of effect. His "Crucifixion" is a remarkable example of his ability to move and impress his auditors with very simple means—and it stands quite unequalled in this respect.

Stainer never attempted a task beyond his powers and contented himself with Church music, for which he had the greatest love and reverence. Since Goss' "O Saviour of the world," no such simple example of pure religious musical expression has come to us as Stainer's "God so loved the world." It was most fittingly sung at the unveiling of a memorial tablet in St. Paul's Cathedral in commemoration of Stainer's great work in rehabilitating the music in that famous fane, and it deeply moved the hearts of all those present on that occasion.

Arthur Seymour Sullivan also deserves a place among the notables of English Church music, although with him it was not a subject that absorbed his entire or perhaps his best attention. He possessed in a high degree the valuble faculty of writing effectively for voices and always avoided unnecessary difficulties. His music is most melodious and singable, but one is at times inclined to feel that the music is of more consequence than the text, and when such is the case it removes the composer from the first rank of excellence.

These three prominent exponents of modern Anglican Church music have been succeeded by a host of younger men, many of whom have marked talent. Such composers as John E. West, George C. Martin, and Villiers Stanford witness to the fact that Church music is very much alive in England to-day and that the artistic quality of the output is not deteriorating. Along with the tremendous development of modern instrumental music, Church music is expanding its borders and drawing upon a wider range of musical material for its expression. More and more demand is made upon the capacity of the singers and the skill of the organist. The organ is no longer a mere support to the voices, but it is treated independently and

vies in importance with the choral parts. Com- Importance of organ part.
posers strive for variety of expression and an
avoidance of the old melodic and harmonic
formulas. In their desire for originality they
not infrequently overstep the mark and write
music that is essentially unvocal. There is a
disposition among the more advanced writers to
treat voices like the wood-wind instruments of
the orchestra, with doublings and criss-crossings
of the parts. Sometimes it is effective and
sometimes it is not. With the multiplication
of musical festivals, the orchestra is used more
and more, and with it comes the temptation to
exploit the instruments rather than the voices.
But with all this exploitation and experiment
there is a distinct gain and without it music as
an art would surely retrograde.

For some years many composers have been Limitations of choral music.
under the impression, if not the conviction,
that all the possibilities in the way of choral
expression have long since been exhausted, and
the most one can hope for is to equal the
efforts of some great master of choral writing
like Bach, Handel, or Mendelssohn. But genius delights in upsetting fixed conclusions and
Edward Elgar and his followers have certainly Edward Elgar (1857 —).
extended the field of choral effects if they have
not actually created new ones. Elgar, in his
large sacred works, has discarded the oratorio
form with its distinct divisions into choruses,

concerted numbers, and solos, and has adopted instead the Wagnerian principle of continuous movement. His one idea is the enhancement of the meaning of the text by every device known to modern music. His "Dream of Gerontius" and more especially his "Apostles" and "The Kingdom" are in reality religious propaganda and must be accepted as such if one is to comprehend their full import. Elgar's methods place his sacred music beyond any suspicion of concert purposes and elevate it to the higher plane of a moral and religious force.

Church music in America.

We are also making progress in America. A half century ago, in the days of the quartette choir, arrangements from secular and sometimes from operatic sources prevailed. Original compositions were weak and poor indeed, being a mixture of mawkish sentimentality and blatant noise. Dudley Buck was the first and almost the only American composer of prominence who wrote especially for the Episcopal Church. Most of his music was intended for the quartette choir and it was a marked advance on anything which had preceded it. Buck's music, while melodious and effective, is however, far removed from the English standards, being less dignified and more emotional—its too frequent cadences giving somewhat of a patchwork effect. His conception of the text is apt to be over-sentimental and his musical expres-

Dudley Buck (1839-1909).

sion of it too literal. The historic canticles of the Church should have breadth and dignity as their prevailing keynote, and anthem texts taken from the Scriptures should have in their musical garb the same high qualities that they have as literature. However, Buck stood more nearly for a distinctive style of American Church music than any other composer and his later works evinced a far higher standard of attainment than his early efforts. The best of them will deservedly remain upon our choir programs for many years to come.

It is only in quite recent years that we have developed Church composers of sufficient ability to compare them favorably with their English contemporaries. Foremost among these is Dr. Horatio Parker, whom Yale has honored with its Chair of Music, and who in turn honors Yale by his pronounced musical gifts. Parker's oratorios and sacred cantatas rank among the most important productions of their kind composed in recent years. They are most highly regarded in England and his "Hora Novissima," as well as other works, have been produced at the great music festivals held in that country. Cambridge has conferred upon him the honorary degree of Doctor of Music, the first instance, so far as the writer is aware, that this signal honor has been conferred upon an American composer. Dr. Parker brings to his

Horatio Parker (1863 —).

Regarded highly in England.

work ripe musicianship, a fertile and inventive imagination, and in addition a penetrating insight into literary values that is all too rare. In addition to his larger works he has written anthems and service numbers, which are all marked by the same fine qualities of force, dignity, and distinctive personality. He always has something of importance to say and says it well. His compositions easily represent the high-water mark of American attainments in the field of Church music, and we, as a nation, may take a just pride in them. We are also indebted to Dr. Parker for his gifts as a teacher and his efforts in this direction have brought forth most excellent fruit.

Arthur Foote, George W. Chadwick, and other prominent American composers have written much excellent Church music, but it has not been especially associated with the Episcopal Church. The list of all those who are doing good and creditable work is too long to mention. Suffice it to say that the average of attainment is slowly improving and that the prospect for the future of Church music in America is at least encouraging.

The preëminence of the English school of Church music is the direct result of centuries spent in systematic efforts to foster and improve religious art. Art in any of its forms cannot flourish without congenial environment, positive ideals, and a stimulating atmosphere. It is of slow growth and attaches itself only to permanent institutions or conditions. Architecture, sculpture, painting, and music all owe their development to the ancient, historic Churches, and the great masterpieces of ecclesiastical art have been wrought out under stress of religious faith and zeal.

If sacred art is to flourish in America it will only develop under the active and coherent efforts of the Church. The growth and expansion of art, particularly music, has been tremendous in recent years, but composers have turned mainly to ancient sagas, folk-lore, the drama, poetry, realism, and idealism for their inspiration. But after all, that which most deeply stirs the souls of men are the things which concern life and death. Faith in the Creator, the hope of heaven, the dread of hell and an abiding realization of what the tragedy on Calvary has signified to a sinful world: these have been the compelling factors which have given us our very greatest art products. The mountain peaks of musical endeavor are still the "Messiah" of Handel, the monumental masses of Bach and Beethoven, the "Requiem" of Mozart, the "Elijah" of Mendelssohn, and the "German Requiem" of Brahms. No operas, no secular cantatas approach them in sublimity or beauty. The highest manifestations of art

Responsibility of the American Church.

must perforce have to do with the most vital things of life.

An American school of Church music.

While certain of our gifted American Church composers have given us works of distinction and well-defined personality, they can scarcely be credited with the creation of an American school of Church music. It is extremely doubtful if such a school can ever arise, for the causes which result in strongly differentiated types of music are rapidly disappearing. Such types are dependent upon isolation, differing habits, traditions, forms of worship, and mental concepts of religion. With the manifold means of intercommunication of modern life, which increase every day, the nations are growing closer and closer, and distinctive characteristics are fast losing their identity. The Church music of the future would seem to be a composite of many styles and many influences. Let us hope it will be a survival of the fittest—a composite of the splendid plainsong of the early Church, the masterly polyphony of the Middle Ages, the classic dignity of the English Cathedral style, plus the richness and fulness of modern art.

BIBLIOGRAPHY

AUTHOR.	TITLE.	CITY.	PUBLISHER.	YEAR.	PRICE.
Archer, Frederick.	The Organ: A Theoretical and Practical Treatise.	London.	Novello.	1875	$2.50
Audsley, Geo. A.	Art of Organ Building. 2 vols., 4to.	New York.	Dodd.	1905	20.00
Barrett, Wm. Alex.	English Church Composers (The Great Musicians Series).	London.	Low.	1882	
Bates, James	Voice Culture for Children. In three parts. (Novello's Music Primers, Nos. 71, 72, 73.)	"	Novello.	Each part,	.75
Bennett, J. G.	The Choir-Boy's Elements of Music. (Novello's Music Primer, No. 64.)	"	"		.75
Benson, L. F.	Studies of Familiar Hymns.	Philadelphia.	Westminster Press.	1898	1.50
Biggs, Louis C.	English Hymnology.	London.	Mozley.	1873	4s.
Bodine, W. D.	Some Hymns and Hymn Writers.	Philadelphia.	Winston.	1907	3.00
Box, Charles	Church Music in the Metropolis.	London.	Reeves.	1884	1.25
Bridge, J. T.	Organ Accompaniment.	"	Novello.	1886	1.00
Briggs, H. B.	The Elements of Plain Song.	"	Quaritch.		3.50

AUTHOR.	TITLE.	CITY.	PUBLISHER.	YEAR.	PRICE.
Buck, Dudley	Illustrations in Choir Accompaniment.	New York.	Schirmer.	1877	3.00
Bumpus, John S.	A History of English Cathedral Music. 2 vols.	"	Pott.	1909	
Charles, Mrs. E. R.	Te Deum Laudamus. Christian Life in Song. The Song and the Singers.	London.	S. P. C. K.	1897	1.50
Church Club of New York.	Lauda Zion: or, The Liturgical Hymns of the Church.	New York.	Young.	1896	.50
Clarke, Wm. H.	Outline of the Structure of the Pipe Organ.	Boston.	Ditson.	1877	1.50
Cowan, Wm., and James Love.	The Music of the Church Hymnary and Psalter in Metre.	Edinburgh.	Froude.	1901	1.25
Crowest, F. J.	The Story of Church Music (announced).	London.	Scott.		1.25
Cummings, W. H.	The Rudiments of Music. (Novello's Music Primer, No. 2.)	"	Novello.		.50
Curwen, John.	Tonic Sol-fa. (Novello's Music Primer, No. 18.)	"	"		.50
Curwen, J. Spencer.	Studies in Worship Music. (1st series, 2d ed.) (2d series.)	"	Curwen.	1888 1885	1.75 1.00
"	The Boy's Voice.	"	"	1894	1.00
D'Esterre-Keeling, Eleonore.	The Story of Bible Music (announced).	"	Scott.		1.25
Dickson, W. E.	Practical Organ Building.	"	Lockwood.	1882	1.25

Author	Title	Place	Publisher	Year	Price
Dickinson, Edw.	Music in the History of the Western Church.	New York.	Scribner.	1902	2.50
Duffield, Samuel W.	English Hymns, their Authors and History.	New York.	Funk.	1886	$3.00
"	The Latin Hymn Writers and their Hymns.	"	"	1889	3.00
Ellis, A. J.	Speech in Song. (Singer's Pronouncing Primer.) (Novello's Music Primer, No. 6.)	London.	Novello.		1.00
Elson, Louis C.	The History of American Music.	New York.	Macmillan.	1904	5.00
Farrow, Miles.	About the Training of Boys' Voices. (A pamphlet.)	"	Young.	1898	.50
Fleming, G. T.	Treatise on Training of Boys' Voices.	London.	Reeves.	1903	.75
Fosbery, C. S.	Chorister's Aid to Monotoning.	"	Novello.		3d.
Foster, Myles Birket.	Anthems and Anthem Composers.	"	"	1901	3.75
Fowler, J. T.	Life and Letters of John Bacchus Dykes.	"	Murray.	1897	3.00
Glass, Henry A.	The Story of the Psalters.	"	Kegan.	1888	
Gregory, A. E.	The Hymn Book of the Modern Church.	"	Kelly Methodist Pub. House.	1904	1.50
Gould, Nat. D.	History of Church Music in America.	Boston.		1853	4.00
Hadow, W. H.	Studies in Modern Music (2 vols.).	New York.	Macmillan.	1894	4.50
Hall, Walter Henry.	The Essentials of Choir-Boy Training.	London.	Novello.	1901	1.00

AUTHOR.	TITLE.	CITY.	PUBLISHER.	YEAR.	PRICE.
Ham, Albert.	A Manual of the Boy's Voice and Its Culture. (A pamphlet.)	London.	Novello.		$ .50
Helmore, Thos.	A Manual of Plain Song for Divine Service. (Also smaller edition by H. B. Briggs.)	"	Frere.	1902	
Hodge, Rev. Charles.	Clergy and Choir.	Milwaukee.	Young Church-man Co.	1891	.50
Hodges, Faustina, H.	Life of Edward Hodges, Organist of Trinity Parish, New York.	New York.	Putnam.	1896	2.50
Hopkins, E. J., and E. F. Rimbault.	The Organ: Its History and Construction.	London.	Cocks.	1877	10.00
Horder, W. Garrett.	The Hymn-Lover: An Account of the Rise and Growth of English Hymnody.	"	Curwen.	1889	
"	The Treasury of American Sacred Song.	"	Frowde.	1896	1.50
Howard, F. E.	The Child Voice in Singing.	New York.	H. W. Gray Co.	1895	.75
"	Handbook on the Training of the Child in Singing.	"	"	1897	.35
Hutchins, A. L.	Annotations of the Hymnal.	Hartford.		1872	
Historical Edition.	Hymns Ancient and Modern.	London.	Wm. Clowes & Sons.	1909	8.75
Johner, Dom Dominic.	A New School of Gregorian Chant.	Ratisbon.	Pustet.	1906	1.00
Jones, F. A.	Famous Hymns and their Authors.	London.	Hodder & Stoughton.	1905	3.00
Julian, John .	Dictionary of Hymnology.	New York.	Scribner.	1892	10.00

King, James.	Anglican Hymnology.	New York.	Pott.	1886	$2.00
Knowles, A.	Text Book of Anglican Service Music from Tallis to J. J. Wesley.	London.	Stock.	1895	.75
Lahee, H. C.	The Organ and Its Masters.	Boston.	Page.	1902	2.00
Latrobe, J. A.	The Music of the Church Considered in its Various Branches.	London.		1831	3.75
Lawrence, Arthur	Sir Arthur Sullivan, Life Story, Letters and Reminiscences.	Chicago.	Stone.	1900	3.50
Lemaistre, A.	A Complete and Practical Method of the Solesmes Plain Chant.	New York.	Wagner.	1904	1.00
Malim, A. W.	English Hymn Tunes from the 16th Century to the Present Times.	London.	Reeves.		.50
Mallinson, Randall.	Choirmasters' Guide to the Selection of Hymns and Anthems for the Service of the Church.	"	Novello.		.75
Martin, Geo. C.	The Art of Training Choir Boys.	"	"	1892	1.50
Matthews, J.	A Handbook of the Organ.	"	Augener.	1897	1.00
Mees, Arthur	Choirs and Choral Music.	New York.	Scribner.	1901	1.25
Messiter, Arthur H.	A History of the Choir and Music, Trinity Church, New York.	"	Gorham.	1906	2.50
Miller, Geo. Laing.	A Recent Revolution in Organ Building.	"	Charles Francis Press.		.25
Miller, Josiah.	Singers and Songs of the Church.	London.	Longmans.	1869	5.00
Mocquereau, Dom André.	Le Nombre Gregorien, ou Rhythmique Gregorienne.	Rome, Tournai.	Desclée et Cie.	1908	Paper, 6fr.

AUTHOR.	TITLE.	CITY.	PUBLISHER.	YEAR.	PRICE.
Moorsome, Robt. M.	Historical Companion to Hymns Ancient and Modern.	London.	Parker.	1889	
Morrison, Duncan.	The Great Hymns of the Church.	"	Simpkins.	1890	1.50
Nicholson, H. D.	Organ Manual. With Directions to Amateurs and Organ Committees.	Boston.	Ditson.		.75
Niedermeyer, Louis, and Joseph D'Ortigue.	Gregorian Accompaniment.	London.	Novello.		1.00
Palgrave, F. T.	The Treasury of Sacred Song.	New York.	Macmillan.	1890	1.50
Powell, Rev. James Baden.	Choralia.	London.	Longmans	1901	1.50
Pratt, Waldo Selden.	Musical Ministries of the Church.	New York.	Revell.	1902	1.00
Prescott, J. E.	Christian Hymns and Hymn Writers.	London.	Bell.	1883	2.40
Richardson, A. Madeley.	Choir Training Based on Voice Production.	"	Novello.	1900	.60
"	Church Music. (Handbook for the Clergy.)	"	Longmans.	1904	.90
Roberts, J. Varley.	A Treatise on a Practical Method of Training Choristers.	"	1st issue. Novello. 2d issue.	1898 1907	2.00
Schaff, Phillip, and Arthur Gilman.	Library of Religious Poetry.	New York.	Funk.	1895	6.00
Smith, Nicholas.	Hymns Historically Famous.	Chicago.	Advance Pub. Co.	1906	1.25
Stainer, John, and Thomas Curry.	The Little Choir Book.	London.	Novello.	1896	.10

Stainer, John.	The Organ Primer. (Novello's Music Primer, No. 3.)	London.	Novello.	1877	1.00
Steele, J. N.	Importance of Musical Knowledge to the Priesthood of the Church.	New York.	Pott.	1895	$ .50
Stubbs, G. Edward.	Congregational Singing.	"	H. W. Gray Co.		.10
"	How to Sing the Choral Service. A Manual of Intoning for the Clergyman.	London.	Novello.	1899	1.00
"	Practical Hints on the Training of Choir Boys.	New York.	H. W. Gray Co.	1898	.75
"	The Adult Male Alto or Counter-Tenor Voice.	"	"	1908	.75
Troutbeck, Rev. J.	Church Choir Training.	London.		1879	.65
Walsh, R. E., and F. G. Edwards.	Romance of Psalter and Hymnal.	New York.	Pott.	1889	2.40
West, John E.	Cathedral Organists, Past and Present.	London.	Novello.		1.50
Williams, C. F. Abby.	The Story of Organ Music.	"	Scott.	1905	1.25
Winkworth, Catherine.	The Christian Singers of Germany.	"	Macmillan.	1869	1.50
Van Broekhoven, J.	The True Method of Voice Production. (For adults.)	New York.	H. W. Gray Co.	1908	1.50

INDEX OF TUNES

GENERAL INDEX